Surviving the Storm
The Life of a Child in Foster Care

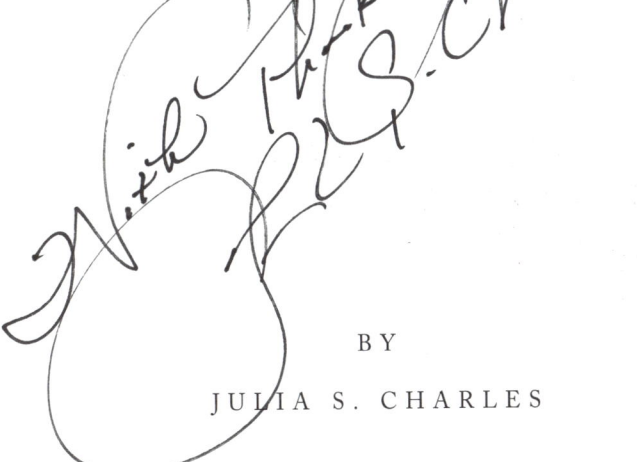

BY
JULIA S. CHARLES

DEDICATION

To Grandma, the late Legolia Lee
The Calm Before The Storm
For listening to my stories before I could write

To Takeya Charles
My Peace Amid the Storm
For all of the laughs that make writing easy

To Mommy, Lorraine Tutt
My Relief after the Storm
For all the memories that make writing worthwhile

TABLE OF CONTENTS

Introduction | The Forecast | page 6

Chapter 1 | The Calm before the Storm | page 9

Chapter 2 | I Hear the Rain | page 15

Chapter 3 | In the Path of Destruction | page 23

Chapter 4 | In the Eye of the Storm | page 33

Chapter 5 | The Aftermath | page 47

Chapter 6 | The Storm is Over | page 63

Chapter 7 | Disaster Relief | page 69

Epilogue | Storm Chasers | page 77

Beyond the Storm | Nancy Carter, ACSW | page 82

Numbers by Julia | page 84

Youth Talk | page 86

Advice for Parents and Caregivers | page 90

Advice for Social Workers and Professionals | page 92

Acknowledgements | page 94

INTRODUCTION
the forecast

Who would have thought that the skinny kid from Virginia would turn out this way? I guess it all started in Portsmouth, Virginia at the Lincoln Park Housing Projects. Life was great. I had my two older brothers and older sister there. We all lived together. I was the baby and my grandparents never let the rest of the family forget it.

It was a fairly warm day and I was outside practicing my skills on a new found hobby; basketball. I had defeated a little girl in the neighborhood who became very angry. She told me, "That's why your Grandmother is going to die. I saw the ambulance in front of your house." Surely she was just angry, I thought. I didn't hear an ambulance, but decided to check just in case. As I walked towards the home, I heard a big commotion. My grandmother was being lifted into the ambulance. My face grew hot with tears. I thought my heart would leap out of my chest. Was it true? Is Grandma going to die?

Have you ever had the feeling that something bad was going to happen and then it does? It's a powerful and scary feeling. I was young, but can recall thinking that life was going to be different from this point.

Have you ever felt so alone and helpless? If you are like me, you have. If you are like me, you understand what it is like to go from complete peace to having it all tossed away with seemingly no regard for the destruction that would ensue. That is what I call a storm.

Storms can occur suddenly without warning or time to prepare. Storms can also come with warnings, but they can still be very unpredictable. Webster's New World Dictionary defines a storm in part as a "sudden strong attack on a fortified place." If you are reading this book and are like me; having grown up in the custody of a Department of Social Services (DSS), then you too should know about storms and fortified places.

Journey with me and find out what it takes to not only survive a storm, but to also become a storm chaser. Experience has taught me to have hope and faith. I no longer mind the storms because I have learned to adjust my sails. I cannot control the way the wind blows, but I can determine how I will respond.

Please understand that I am work in progress. I am not where I would like to be. But I am certainly further along than where I used to be. I'm moving towards my goals. I seek to find my true self and purpose. Along the way, I will continue to adjust to the storms and discover myself.

CHAPTER 1
the Calm before the Storm

Have you ever noticed that before a big storm hits, the air is usually still? I call it a state of peace. That stillness is common in real life and with the environment. It was the case for me as well. Life could not have been better...before the storm.

I lived in a home "jammed packed" with relatives. My grandparents, three older siblings, an aunt and her three children, an uncle, three cousins and I all lived together in the Lincoln Park housing projects. All of us; in one house! Considering the number of people, it never seemed crowded. We had so much fun. I remember all the children in our home playing with neighborhood kids until the street lights shined. The Saturday night parties were the best. They were just like on TV. My aunts and older cousins had their friends over to play cards and listen to music, while the children played games in the back room. Every once in a while my aunt yelled for my cousin to come and dance for her company.

Sunday dinners were the pinnacle of family gatherings. My grandmother started dinner before church. The food cooked the entire time we were in service. This in itself was amazing. We were often in church from nine in the morning until three in the afternoon. *Yes that is a long time!* Fried chicken, black-eyed peas, macaroni and cheese, collard greens, yeast rolls; you name it, and it was on the dinner table any Sunday, or weekday for that matter. There was never enough room at the dinner table, but somehow we always made due.

The best part of life in Virginia was being my grandmother's baby. It was awesome to get up early, run into her bedroom, and kiss her soft cheeks. She was always so busy; it seemed to me she never slept. She was beautiful. Even as a kid, I could see that. I remember thinking people like Grandma are too good to be true. When our family argued, she would always make sure we made up. She was so forgiving that it sometimes made me angry. Loving her as much as I did, I did not want to see her hurt, sad, or even frustrated. I could remember everyone who raised their voices or rolled their eyes at her because there were so few. She was the only person that I knew that everyone loved and I could not wait to see her everyday.

It was almost two in the morning when I heard a knock on the door. It was my older brother, Michael. He was around fourteen years old, I was six. He had been in North Carolina all summer. My grandmother told me earlier that day that Michael was spending the summer with our mother. She mentioned he was coming back that night. So I decided to stay awake for him. He was very happy to see my grandmother and the rest of the family. I guess Michael really missed Grandma considering she had raised him for many years prior to his leaving for the summer. Michael grabbed her with a big hug. While everyone moved about welcoming him home, I noticed a fairly sizeable woman walking into the room. She was no taller than 4'11". What she lacked in height she made up in width. She took a seat on the couch and talked about all the things my brother had done during the summer. This woman made it sound as if he had gone to the happiest place on earth. She told us how Michael had gotten a job shining shoes at the furniture market in High Point, North Carolina. My brother finally told me who she was. She was my mother—Lena.

I had sometimes tried to imagine what my mother looked like. I imagined a face to match the voice that I occasionally heard over the phone. There were even times when I looked up at an airplane and waved as if she were on board. I can even recall being bullied once in kindergarten and crying desperately for my mother. I always had Grandma and I would not trade her for anything in the world. But in my mind, there is certain sadness about a child who does not have a mother.

My heart needed her…

I needed to hear that she loved me…

I needed to hear that I was special to her…

I didn't even care at this point why she was not in my life. There was a pit of anxiety in my stomach when I realized the woman standing before me was my mother. The woman I had imagined for so long. If my grandmother was the world's greatest grandmother then certainly my mother would be the world's greatest mother, right?

I looked at her and took in her features. Lena looked nothing like I imagined, but she had a beautiful smile. I knew little about her. I wasn't even sure if I should call her "Mom." As I looked at her, I was a little disappointed and realized beyond our complexions, we looked nothing alike. Lena was a short, portly woman with beautiful dark skin. She was the first person with dark skin, besides my little cousin, that I considered beautiful. Dark skin was automatically negative in my eyes. This is sort of ironic considering I have dark skin too.

Not long after school started in the fall Grandma went back into the hospital. This time she was there for a long time. Granddaddy, my siblings, and I went to see her everyday after school. We walked into Maryview Hospital and went straight to her room. My grandmother soon expected to see us everyday. I walked in every day eager to tell her what had happened in my fourth grade class. Because I was so tiny, I would sit on the bed and plait her hair. She looked ridiculous with a head of unsightly plaits, but she left them in because her "baby" had done her hair. We normally stayed a few hours after school and then went home. While Grandma was in the hospital, I spent most of my days watching everyone else do stupid things at school so I had something to tell her that afternoon. In hindsight, I'm sure I talked way too much, but she never seemed to tire of my stories or stupid questions.

Then one day, just like everyday, it was time to leave. We kissed Grandma the way we always did, and told her how much we loved her. "See you tomorrow," we told her as we left. If I knew that was the last time I would see Grandma on this earth, my "I love you" would have been more than just a habitual one. I would have kissed her a little longer. I would have made it a point to fall asleep in her arms. I would have carefully braided her hair to make her look nice rather than to release my nervous energy. If I knew that was the last time I would see my best friend alive, I would have told her more about my day than just about the girl I didn't like at school. I would have told her all the things I should tell a best friend. I would have gently hugged her neck until my little arms were exhausted. I would have laid my ear against her chest and kept time to the rhythm of her heartbeat. I would have absorbed every smell that would later remind me of her; like the smell of her hair or the smell of her housecoat after cooking dinner. I would have captured every moment in a photograph so that I would never forget the shape of her nose or the shine in her eyes. The only picture I have of her does not even belong to me. Every once in a while I look at that picture of us and remember how real my smile was then; before it was disfigured by life's suffering. If I had known she was leaving me, I would have made conversation matter; instead of spewing meaningless babble about my insignificant fourth grade life.

My Grandma always taught me that God knew what He was doing all the time. At that time, I did not believe her. I believe her now but the pain and sadness I felt had a way of destroying my hope and faith. It was hard to imagine I would ever have hope or faith again.

Don't you hate it when you leave the house not expecting showers and then it rains and you get caught without an umbrella or a raincoat? I realized that I have to be proactive and check the forecast. Preparation can determine how to adjust to the storm. Lack of preparation can change plans and create chaos.

I woke up for school the next day and while we were getting dressed my uncle called everyone into the living room. We sat on the couches and waited for him to speak. I looked at Granddaddy. He had his head in his hands. My uncle told us he was sorry, but Grandma was not coming home anymore. Just as he finished speaking, my brother and sister burst into tears. My oldest brother jolted out of the house. He was very angry at what my uncle said. I did not understand why everyone was so upset. Sure, I thought, we wanted Grandma to come home, but if that was not possible, we would see her in the hospital just the way we had been for weeks. I told my uncle it was okay and shared my thought about visiting her in the hospital. Suddenly, Granddaddy started crying; gut wrenching sobs that were too painful to hear. It was like something on the inside was hurting him and he couldn't get it out. When I saw him cry, everything started to become clear. This was bad news. I never saw Granddaddy cry before that day. I knew then something was terribly wrong. Granddaddy was a big man. He stood about 6'4" and weighed two hundred fifty pounds or more. He was quite a "manly man." What was wrong? What were they trying to tell me? Why couldn't I go and see Grandma at the hospital?

It took me a few hours to realize I was never going to braid Grandma's hair again. I was never going to sit on the bed and talk about our favorite TV show, *Good Times*. I was never going to hear her say, "Come hug my neck." I was never again going to taste her fresh baked yeast rolls. She was the glue in our family. Who was going to solve all our family's problems? What about the community? Who was going to take up the slack as the "candy lady" in our neighborhood? I was only nine years old at the time. I was too young to understand the impact her death would have on our family. It seemed that as soon as Grandma died, we stopped having Sunday dinners and all my family members moved out of our house. Even at my age, I sensed life was about to change.

I stood alone in the living room. The house seemed to close in around me. For a moment, I could not breathe. I was in shock. My little nine year old mind could not grasp that Grandma would never come home again. The worst part was that I could not see her anymore. Who was going to cook French toast on Saturday morning? Who was going to wash clothes and hang them out to dry? Who was going to tell us to "stop running in and out of my house?" And who was going to tell us to shut the front door because "I can't afford to air condition the whole neighborhood?" My mind was boggled. I thought of all the things I could have said. I wished for a chance to relive the previous few weeks before her death.

Finally, I walked up the stairs into my grandmother's bedroom. My grandfather was sitting in his chair. He was still in shock. His blood-shot eyes and swollen cheeks told me he had cried even more. I was so sad for him. I realized I lost my best friend, but so had he. It was more about a friend than a housekeeper and chef.

Later that night, all the children sat in the back room while the adults planned the funeral. I also heard a discussion about how the family planned to handle my siblings and me. Who was going to take all four of us? Finally an aunt suggested that someone call our biological mother. After all, they said, we belonged to her and why should they have to deal with all her children. I walked into the living room just as the conversation was getting heated. It wasn't that they didn't want us. *So they said.* It was just the reality of the situation. They were saying it was time for my mother to grow up and take care of her own children. With that, a phone call was made and my mother, Lena was on her way to Virginia. She was coming for the funeral to say goodbye to her mother, but she would be leaving with a whole lot more.

The calm was over, it was about to rain and here I stood without an umbrella to shield my heart.

CHAPTER 2
I hear the Rain

When a thunderstorm is approaching, sometimes it can be heard. I was once told that the number of seconds between hearing thunder and seeing lighting is approximately the number of miles between me and a storm. I am not sure how accurate that formula is, but a similar gauge in my personal life would be awesome! Then I would know to get prepared for "rain" and not get caught in the storm – which could ruin everything.

One gloomy Monday morning I ran a few miles in a conditioning class at school. I was so upset because I was not prepared. I had just gotten my hair done over the weekend. I never expected to physically exert myself. The only reason I chose the class was because it was rumored to be full of men. I just wanted to wear my cute work-out clothes and not actually work out; especially not after I had just gotten my hair done. It had nothing to do with ability; after all I had been an athlete in years prior. I had the stamina to run a few miles, but what I lacked was an umbrella. I decided to suck it up and run mainly because my grade depended on it.

I walked outside with the rest of the class and was met by a pesky constant drizzle. I was livid. I knew my hair was going to be a wreck by the end of the run. I had a bad attitude but now I was in the middle of it, so I kept running. The farther I ran alongside the parkway, the harder it rained. I was soaked. The money I spent on my hair was officially wasted. What was I going to do with my hair now? I couldn't afford to get it done again, so now what? This taught me to always keep a spare umbrella or rain hood. Understand, I am not asking the rain to stop. I am simply asking that it not ruin my hair. The rain hood would have safeguarded me (and my hair) from the rain, and at the same time kept the plants happy. A win-win situation. I know rainy days will come; I just had to learn to be prepared.

After the funeral, my mother packed our things and we were headed to High Point, North Carolina. The ride to my new home was quite surreal. I couldn't believe I was leaving the only family I had known, to live with a woman I had barely met. I was trading my Virginia friends for more siblings waiting in North Carolina. Siblings I had never spoken with for more than a few minutes. Oh, the rain was coming. I could feel it coming. Only moments away and I was going to get caught – without an umbrella once again.

High Point did not look much different than the housing projects I left. It was a little cleaner and a lot less violent. There was no "candy lady," but besides that, the towns were practically the same. Shortly after we moved to North Carolina my mother left her nice three bedroom, two bathroom home for a five bedroom, two bathroom house leased by the local housing authority. Needless to say she was enraged… with us; her children. Not only had she lost her mother, but in her mind, we (her children) ruined her life. We caused her to endure the humility of being on welfare.

Have you ever heard the saying, "When it rains, it pours?" That is so true for many people and it seems to be the story of my childhood. Lena had challenges and frustrations dealing with the "new" children. Part of me understands because she went from a comfortable life of raising three children to raising seven children almost over night. It seemed she hated us, and in my little mind, she hated me in particular. I feared her miserably. That fear grew in me almost daily.

I can recall not being able to focus at school for fear I had left the lights on at home. What if she went home for lunch and saw the lights on? If so, I was sure to "get it" when I got home; thankfully I usually remembered to turn them off.

Over the next few months, the siblings I knew so well before our move, became totally different people. My oldest brother, Michael, used to enjoy hanging out at home with the family in Virginia. Now he was hardly ever home. He had new friends that consumed most of his time. In hindsight, I wondered if he stayed away simply because he was a teenager and preferred his friends over family. At the time however; I was convinced he stayed with friends because of what was happening at home. I figured he did not like our new arrangement and had his own way to avoid it. Perhaps I projected my feelings onto him. Truthfully, I never asked him; it was always easier for me to assume. Part of me hated that he was not there with me. I was angry with him. He was always there for me back home in Virginia. Why not now? I soon learned that he would always be there for me when it counted.

My older sister, Justice, changed too. She had been an outgoing kid with a smile that lit up the world, and now she was a sad and fearful girl, forced to become a woman and maintain a home at the ripe old age of ten. She even became angry and "jumpy" all of sudden. The smallest little thing would make her angry and frustrated.

The death of Grandma was still fresh when we enrolled at school in High Point. Justice went to class with a boy who was quite the class clown. While cracking jokes one day he mentioned something about Grandma. Despite his joking nature, my sister "flipped out" (got really mad). Justice was so hurt by her classmate's comments and she proceeded to beat up the boy. (Grandmothers should never be made into a joke.) When Justice was suspended, my mother believed it was intentional so that she could stay home and "mess with some little boy." My sister suffered a double blow that day; not only had she gotten into a fight defending Grandma, but she was suspended and accused of having ulterior motives. She had never been suspended before. I could see an immediate difference in her attitude from that point. She quickly developed an "I-don't-care" attitude. She never intentionally got into trouble in the house, but it was unavoidable. I could tell she felt that no matter what she did, she would get into trouble; which is a difficult place for a child to be.

When children get to a point where they have been disciplined so much that it does not hurt anymore, they are much more likely to get into trouble. They are also more likely to talk back and misbehave. Imagine trying to do things right and still being punished? I am an advocate of discipline within reason; discipline should match the behavior. Be aware; when a child does not care, like Justice was, a parent needs to be concerned.

The biggest transformation besides me was my other brother, Marcus. He was a carefree little boy who was becoming silent, resentful, and a downright angry kid. He barely spoke anymore – to anyone. I was so afraid for him. No one ever asked Marcus how he felt when Grandma passed. I still think he never really got over it. Grandma was his mother for many years. Now who was going to bring him out of his shell? Who was going to be interested in him? Marcus and Justice shared the same smile. Marcus, who used to be full of laughter, now spent his time memorizing information on the back of baseball cards. I was convinced that he was traumatized by my grandmother's death and the move. He was only interested in memorizing statistics of his favorite players and nothing beyond that. Life had no meaning. He didn't bother anyone and no one bothered him. I wish someone important had asked him how he felt. I wanted someone to tell Marcus they cared about him; my mother never told him, "I love you."

The pain of loosing Grandma and having mother physically abuse him must have been too much for Marcus to handle, and he did not have an *umbrella*. Grandmother had a way of making each grandchild feel as if they were the only person that mattered in the entire world. All the grandchildren had a special bond with her. Marcus was probably affected more than anyone else in the entire family. He was the one who never cried no matter how hard he was hit. He barley flinched by my mother's blows, but that doesn't mean he escaped pain.

I also was impacted by our move to North Carolina. Notably, I was no longer the baby and I went from the beautiful (at least in Grandma's eyes) child who could do no wrong to a sneaky, defiant, hateful, miserable, ugly, vindictive, and truly sad little girl. This was the first time I can recall ever being genuinely and totally unhappy as a child. Unfortunately, this time of misery and discontent was long-term. I missed Grandma more with each passing day, each verbal criticism, and especially with each relentless weighty hand across my body.

Things were different now. It seemed that I could do nothing right. I remember one day when I was told to clean the bathroom. Apparently, my younger siblings who had been living with my mother, already knew how to clean, and that we (older children) were stupid and never taught how to clean properly. There I was, on my knees leaning across the bathtub, scrubbing it with a sponge. I never even saw her coming until it was too late. The wooden broom handle landed across my scrawny back. The first blow was unbelievable. I lunged forward as the wood struck me. The lashes were seemingly unending to my nine year old body. I could not wait for it to end. I cried in agony wanting the blows to stop. After awhile, I think I must have become numb to the pain - crying became more of a reflex than a response to pain.

When it was all over, I just laid there. Did she really think that after this I would have the energy to clean the stupid bathtub? I was so angry. I cried into the night. I knew I could never say anything to her. I was so upset and truly hurt. I cried myself to asleep. This began my method for ending most beatings - sleeping became my escape.

A few days and several whippings later, I listened as my older sister performed her chores. She was slated to iron all the clothes for everyone in the house - clothes for seven children and two adults! I remember that as she was midway through the job, she noticed a wrinkle on one of the items that she had already ironed. Naturally, Justice gave the spot another "once over" with the iron. As she did that, my "new" little sisters walked in and promptly told my mother that Justice ironed the clothes wrong. They told her my sister ironed clothes after putting them on the hanger. Naturally Lena was enraged. She called Justice all kinds of names from lazy and dumb to sneaky. She proceeded to drive this point home with a few brutal blows to my sister. I wondered why Lena didn't just take a look at the rest of the clothes; at least then she would have seen that Justice really did iron the other clothes properly. I remember wishing my mother would beat me instead of my sister. I wished I could take at least a few blows for her. It made me angrier to watch Justice get beaten than when I was on the receiving end. I was furious with the sister who had lied to Lena. I thought siblings were supposed to stick up for each other, not "rat" on each other.

The following months were outrageous. I was such an unhappy kid, no one wanted to be around me. I do not blame them. I was a miserable child and being with me was no fun at all. I was no longer my former, happy, jovial self. Life was so much easier when I could slip into my dream land; at least there Grandma was waiting and even happy to see me. I wanted to sleep long and often because then I could still kiss Grandma and tell her goodnight. In my dreams sometimes I could ask her if we (her grandchildren) did something to make her leave; but I always woke up before I got a response.

It was winter now and strong physical discipline had become common place. Justice somehow dropped the mailbox key outside in the snow and was having trouble finding it. She explained to Lena that while running to the mailbox she slipped and fell on the ice. The keys fell out of her hand and were washed down the drain. Lena insisted the keys were still outside and sent her to look in the snow with nothing on her hands. Justice went outside for what seemed like forever with a metal spoon digging the snow searching for the keys. I watched as my mother went outside and grabbed the spoon from her hand and slapped her across the face with it. I was in shock as the blood ran from my sister's mouth. This was mean, even for Lena. I was beyond angry. I was furious. It was an accident. Lena made mistakes too. Why was she so unforgiving when her children made mistakes? Not long after that my sister went to school and didn't come home.

I was angry and hurt that Justice went to school and did not return. I was sitting in the living room when Lena received the phone call that my sister was not coming home until Child Protective Services (CPS) could investigate her claims. I was upset, but more than that, I was jealous. Why would she leave me there? She knows that the oldest girl in the house gets in the most trouble. With Justice gone, I was the oldest girl. I would never have left her. I missed her already and an entire day had not yet passed. I needed her. Whose bed was I going to climb in at night? That was our special bond. Now the other side of the bed was left cold; just as cold as her decision to leave me there alone. More than that, I did not have her strength. I was a real weakling and now the oldest girl in the house, therefore slated for the brunt of the beatings.

I was angry with Justice for quite a while until one day Justice and a social worker called. The social worker wanted to know if the claims my sister made about my mother were true. Of course they were valid, my sister was telling the truth, but there was a problem. The social worker called my house. If I told the real truth, I would be brutally punished. Amid conversations about abuse, my mother sat next to me. She coached my words with threats. I was asked; in my eyes had my sister really been abused? Of course she had. What should I do? What would you do in that situation? I was jealous that my sister was free and I was not. I was infuriated that she called CPS and compromised my safety in order to solidify her freedom. I did what anyone in my situation would do. I lied. I simply told the social worker my sister had lied about everything. As I spoke, I silently hoped I had not caused Justice to be returned home. No matter how envious I was of her new situation, I would never wish the pain I was feeling at that time on her. I hoped she would understand that I had to lie.

It only took me a few weeks to realize Justice had to leave when she did. I forgave her in my heart for leaving me. This life was survival of the fittest. When you find a way out, take it. Not everyone can be a Harriet Tubman. Some people have to find their way to freedom on their own. Whether freedom is found through the help of someone like Harriet Tubman, who returned to lead others, or an escape is found and taken individually, at the end of the day freedom is achieved. That is what people seek, freedom. In my case, I wanted freedom so badly I could taste it. I often dreamt of a day when I could leave and never return. I saw myself back in Virginia with my family. Then I awoke in tears, realizing I was only dreaming and none of those things were reality. Reality was the most painful thing I endured. Knowing someone else knew the route to achieve freedom and I was… still bound.

The irony with rain is while some loath it, others look forward to it. Some even need it. I once heard that in desperation for rain, Native Americans created the Rain Dance. This dance is performed believing the gods would appreciate the dance and bless the land with rain. Some say rain was inevitable; the dance helped to endure the wait. Other's say the dance was successful because it ended only when rain came. Native Americans embody a faith that requires patience and a belief that relief is on the way.

Another aspect of rain is it never falls on just one person's house. So naturally when it rained in my life it affected more than just me. Many people felt the rain. While I understand the rain will eventually assist personal growth, I would rather not be drenched.

CHAPTER 3

in the path of Destruction

Have you ever seen the movie *Twister*? There is a scene when the two main characters are in the direct line of a devastating whirlwind. They are faced with a dilemma and they must act quickly. Should they run out the storm in their vehicle or should they find refuge and safety in the nearest ditch? Life is about to change for the characters and they know it. It is so weird when you sense that life is about to change. I can sometimes feel it in the pit of my stomach. It is like being at the height of a rollercoaster that is about to drop at gut-wrenching speed. Nothing can be done to stop it. Electing to get off the ride is not an option. One can only stay on the ride, scream and see what happens next. That is sort of what life was like for me right before the big move into foster care.

When I lived with my mother, we occasionally went to Sunday school. The teachers told us a story about Jesus out on a boat with his disciples. There was a great wind storm with waves that beat the ship. The boat filled with water. Jesus was awoken by his disciples. As the story goes, Jesus arose, scolded the wind, and said to the sea, "Peace - be still." At that the wind ceased, and there was a great calm.

I wished I had the power to speak to my storm. At the sound of my voice, it would cease, and I would be happy. It was many years before I learned the power of my decisions and words along with the impact they had on my experiences and relationships.

One night I went into the kitchen to help with dinner. My mother stood at the stove with the oven door open. A few seconds later as she checked the meat and accidentally dropped the fork into the oven between the racks. She grabbed me by the arm and told me to get it out. I was smart enough to know the oven was hot. I reached into the sink to get a towel in order to move the racks and not burn myself. As I reached for the racks, I was slapped across the face. I was shocked. My mother said, "Who told you to get a towel?" She then went on to say, that my arms were small enough to reach under the rack without getting burned. She added that if I got burned, then I would get into trouble. I silently refused and was surprised to not get a whipping; that is until later. That night as I was getting out of the shower, I was met with a switch. The sting was not nearly as hard as her hand, so I took it. The damage however was far more lasting because my skin had been softened by the water. My legs bled at first, but eventually stopped. As I dried off, I noticed marks all over my legs that would become scars lasting a few days or even weeks. No one must know. I would tell no one. Everyday I rubbed Vaseline on my legs. I am not sure if it helped my scars or not; but at least I felt like it did.

I wore pants for a while after that incident otherwise people would begin to ask questions. My mother did not give me the *"What goes on in the house, stays in the house"* speech, but I knew better then to mention anything that went on in that house. So everyday for a week or so, I privately tended to my wounds before getting dressed. It took longer than expected for my wounds to heal because my jeans created friction against my legs. The rubbing against my scars caused them to bleed again and again.

Often times after receiving a whipping, I looked at my older brother with desperation. *Help me! Please save me!* I was so tiny and my body could not handle such rough treatment. I know Marcus felt bad that he did not help me sooner. Back home in Virginia he always made sure I was okay (I was the baby remember?). Now I was no longer the baby, but knew he still felt responsible to keep me safe. Now, Marcus just got angry. Every time I was "disciplined," Marcus got angrier. After all it was his job to protect a "Charles," a real member of the family, at all cost and now he was being defeated.

A few weeks later my legs healed so I took the initiative and help with groceries. It was really more of an expectation than initiative. As I unpacked the groceries, I heard my mother yelling for my siblings and me to help with the rest of the groceries. I responded and unpacked the remainder of the cans placing them in the cupboard. As I finished I noticed my mother behind me, undoubtedly to scrutinize my work. She mentioned that there was a system to the way that she kept her groceries. I remember being hit a few times with a plastic bag containing several cans. The pain seemed larger than life. I cried from the depth of my heart. I screamed from the pit of my stomach until there was nothing left. Days like that made me miss my sister the most. I wondered if she knew what was happening to me. I imagined her somewhere safe while I was tormented. Was she more concerned about her safety than mine? Could I blame her if she was?

Physical discipline had become common place, almost normal. I could handle the spankings, but in my mind it was outlandish. Whatever happened to being "popped" or even spanked on the bottom? Here at eleven years old, I thought my own mother, was trying to kill me. Truthfully, I often wished she would just kill me. At least if I were dead, I would no longer feel pain. After all, she never said she loved me (like Grandma did all the time), in fact, she downright disliked me and made it known. In reality the likelihood that she was truly trying to kill me was slim, but a child in this situation could certainly make that assumption.

How could my mother and grandmother be so different? I remember my mother saying that we were the reason Grandma died. That comment hurt much more than any beating I ever experienced. Whoever said, "Sticks and stones make break my bones, but words will never hurt me," must have been super human to not be effected by words. I would rather be beaten to death than told I was the reason Grandma died. The tongue is so powerful. If I am constantly told I am ugly, stupid, or I caused my Grandmother's death, I could eventually believe it. When someone continually speaks disapproving words, especially someone that matters, those words become real and impact your life. That was my life. I was always called black, ugly, stupid, and other demeaning words. For years, I learned to resent anyone who said the opposite of what I had come to believe about myself.

The same day as I lay on the kitchen floor recovering from my "bag" whipping, I wondered why she hated me. She was at least humane to the others.

What did I do to make her feel this way?

How could I change to make her love me?

I cried at the thought that I repulsed her. Only this time when I cried, it was different. It hurt… a lot. I wept from my soul. I wept from an internal place. I had never been so deep, even when Grandma passed. A reserve of tears came voluntarily down my face. I began to converse with God for the first time in my life. "God, I quit," I said, deeply hurt that He had not yet come to my aid and I was in the middle of a storm just like His disciples. After all, my Grandma used to say, "He's an on-time God." I understood that meant when I needed Him, He would be there in the nick-of-time. "I give up God. I don't want to do this anymore." I resolved as stupid and childish as it may sound, to take my last breath. I closed my eyes and begged God to take me. My tears stopped. Life and this torture were not worth it anymore.

At that moment Marcus came into the kitchen and said, "If you get up I promise I will get you out of here. I promise." The look in his eyes offered hope. Hope I believed was non-existent. He meant what he said. I still thought he was too late. I looked at him and saw he wanted me to live. He wanted me to survive. I saw he loved me. He really loved me. That love helped me go the distance. I had longed for love since the day I met my mother. I thought my desire for her love was just a strong yearning. I was wrong. Love was a need. My brother filled that nothingness in my heart with a few words. That was enough.

I wish I could convey my feelings over the next few weeks. Everyday offered a new optimism. I felt hope. Each sunrise suggested that life was not yet over. It seemed to announce that I was one step closer to liberation from my personal prison. I was energized by my faith that freedom was at hand. My brother gave me hope through love.

A few weeks after my brother made his promise, Child Protective Services (CPS) started an investigation. The CPS worker came to school, requested to meet with me and my siblings, and asked us questions. At first I thought the situation was reminiscent of when the social worker called on behalf of my older sister. How could I possibly tell the truth when my younger siblings were in the room listening? They would surely tell my mother everything I said to that CPS worker. So, again, I lied. I was sure that I messed it up for my brothers who were not afraid to tell the truth. But I was terrified. If I got beat relentlessly for not arranging the cans properly in the cupboard, surely my mother would kill me if she learned I was not on her side.

Eventually, I was able to talk to the CPS worker by myself. I sat in an office and sang like a canary. I told her everything. I felt excited to get everything off of my chest. I then noticed she was writing as I spoke and became afraid.

What did she write?

What would she do with her paper?

Was she going to show my mother this report?

I could not wait to get home and tell my big brother that I had finally told the truth.

I walked into the house that afternoon. Before I said anything my brother told me someone was coming to get us. He told me to make sure that I got him when the "people" arrived at our house. A few hours later there was a knock at the door. I looked out the window and saw two police cars and a plain car with the county symbol on it. I ran to the bathroom to get my brother. I warned him that all hell was about to break loose. By the time he came out of the bathroom, the social worker was already in the living room handing my mother a stack of papers.

My mother was enraged. She started yelling at me about things she read in the report. One police officer took me by the hand. He escorted me to my bedroom and instructed me to grab some clothes. As I packed my things, my mother yelled at what not to take. The worker told my mother that with counseling our family could be "reunified" in a minimal amount of time. Well, my mother would have no part of counseling. She said, "If y'all think you can do better, take 'em and I don't want 'em back." I was hurt and relieved all at the same time. I knew that once I left I was gone. I did not care if she did everything they told her to do. I would die before I lived with her again.

That same night as we sat in the office of the High Point Department of Social Services I looked at my brothers and no longer felt peace. The office was so cold, stark and unwelcoming. I was worried. I listened to the Social Worker try to locate a family for three children—two of whom were teenagers. Even I knew no one was going to take teenagers. The social worker looked at me. Although she assured me that we would be placed together, my heart was no longer calm. I wondered if I would ever see my brothers again after that night.

As I sat there, I memorized my brothers' features just in case I would have to find them later in life. They had been such a major part of me. I had already lost my best friend (Grandmother) and a big sister. I sensed I was about to lose them too. I never experienced a goodbye that hurt so much. When my grandmother passed away, she was no longer alive, so I knew that was a permanent goodbye. This goodbye was more painful because my big brothers were alive; I just could not see or be with them. I was almost angry with God, blaming Him for cutting off my sibling lifeline - the same lifeline that offered me hope. I was in complete turmoil as I waited for an available family. It was late that night when the social worker tried to tell me I would no longer live with my brothers anymore.

I sat in the back of the county car in route to a foster home completely livid and almost lifeless. Who was going to protect me now? I was only eleven and now I had to care for myself. Who was I going to call when life got hard? When I couldn't sleep, whose bed would I climb into now? My life was utterly destroyed! I thought of all the things I had been through in recent years; loosing Grandma, being abused, wanting to die, and now this. I thought of all those things and felt tired. What was going to happen next? My mind was overwhelmed with ideas and projections of what was about to happen. I immediately plummeted into the abyss of depression.

We arrived at the foster home and I walked up to the door. With a trash bag full of my belongings, I rang the doorbell. An interracial couple came to the door and embraced me. I was taken aback by their forwardness. This was uncomfortable. I could not wait for the hug to be over. The middle-aged black woman, Ms. April, showed me to my room. I did not get a tour of the house that night. After the social worker left, my foster mother closed the door behind her and said it was time for me to go to sleep. Everything was so new. This is foster care? What had I gotten myself into? The trees outside the bedroom window seemed to come alive. The sounds of the night were unfamiliar so every noise made me jump. Who could sleep in a place like this? I sat in the corner of the room and cried all my tears. I just wanted my family back. Life was different… again. What I didn't realize is that I entered the foster care system with an advantage. You see I was a "Charles" and there is inherent nobility in that name. We are resilient. We make it through anything. I just did not know it but apparently it was brewing within me.

For some strange reason, I wanted to return to my mother. It was odd to want to return to the one who beat me, didn't love me, and made me live in fear. Ironically, the "tyrant" did not seem as fearful as this new situation. I now tell my friends that when on the brink of freedom, do not go back into bondage regardless of the unknown ahead. At least the unknown path is leading somewhere, further from bondage and closer to freedom. But it is hard to trust the unknown. That night, in the corner of my new room, I cried. I wondered how I arrived at this place. Until recently I had never cried so much. I was really getting tired of crying. I did not even know where the bathroom was in this house. I opened the door and looked down the hall. The pictures that hung on the walls seemed to come alive. The people in the pictures were asking who I was and why I was there. In fear, I closed the door. I sat in the corner again and held my bladder as long as I could. Eventually, I urinated right there in the corner and fell asleep.

I woke up the next morning to get ready for school. I was so embarrassed that I slept in a puddle of urine. I went to school certain all my teachers knew what happened the previous day. I was so upset by the way I was treated once the news spread through the faculty. Before entering foster care, I thoroughly enjoyed school. But now, I saw an immediate change in my teachers. They did not appear to care as much as they did previously. I became an invisible student in their classes. Whenever I raised my hand I was ignored. I could feel a stigma attached to my name. I was no longer just Julia Charles. Now I was Julia Charles, "the foster child." I was now a statistic and fully conscious of this fact in the early stages of my journey through foster care.

Everything was spiraling out of control. I was consumed by circumstances and feeling unable to do anything about my situation. I spoke to no one because after all opening my mouth was what got me here in the first place. If I could find one thing to control, I would be fine. I could not control where I lived. I could no longer control my relationships with my teachers. They now had ideas about me. There had to be something that was mine. Something I could control myself. It took me a few days after I moved to realized there was something I could control - food.

The idea hit me like a ton of bricks. I ate when I wanted and no one could make me do otherwise. I crept, instantaneously, yet quietly, into the world of anorexia. It took years and many lost pounds before anyone realized this was an issue for me.

In order for me to control my food, I had to hide it and make life appear normal. This was my personal thing and I had to keep it secret. I had to make is so no one could even suspect it. Initially, I just lost my appetite. I was never really hungry anyway. Eventually, I taught myself to think of other things when I felt the urge to eat. Abstinence from food quickly became my cry for help. One would think that someone would care enough to ask me what was wrong - no one ever did. The people who were supposed to notice never did. My social workers changed repeatedly so no one was ever around long enough to know how I previously looked. The school nurse was not used to me yet, so she was clueless. To everyone else I made sure it appeared that I ate normal portions. I often moved food around on my plate which made it look like I had eaten. No one noticed. I made sure I kept my mouth shut and my actions inconspicuous. Years went by before I realized the detriment I caused to my body. Even today, eating on a daily basis is a challenge. I have to be persistent in my pursuit to stay healthy. I was hurting myself. Although I felt completely destroyed, I was still alive. My story could not end there. I turned inward and tried to make sense of my mess. Where would I find hope now? Is faith an option? I felt abandoned by everyone including my grandmother's God.

CHAPTER 4

in the eye of the Storm

Have you noticed that the eye of a storm does not differ too much from the human eye? Each part of the human eye serves an essential purpose in a person's ability to see. For example, the eyebrow serves as the eye's natural visor against the sun. Eyelashes filter dust and foreign objects so nothing blocks the vision. And the eyelids cover the eyeball; the center of the eye. If you try to touch the eye, the lids blink instinctively to protect it. All external parts of the eye are designed to protect the center and keep it safe. The safety of the eyeball allows for clear vision.

The eye of the storm is no different. The swirling winds, temperature, and water of the storm circle the eye. This movement builds energy to maintain the strength required to keep the eye of the storm calm and safe. So while tremendous activity was surrounding the eye, it was protected. I was soon to discover what was protecting me.

It had been a few months since I entered foster care. I lived in several respite homes (temporary, short-term homes) until a long-term foster home could be found. On the night of my twelfth birthday, I went to live with a Caucasian woman. This was my first long-term foster home.

I walked in with my trusty trash bag and placed it on the floor. My social worker never even came inside. I introduced myself to Ms. Emily. She greeted me as she finished her make-up in the mirror. I asked, "Ms. Emily, where are we going?"

"We aren't going anywhere. I am going to dinner with some colleagues from the local house of representatives," she commented.

I had no idea what she was talking about, but whatever it was it must have been important. There was an air of arrogance about her.

"What am I going to do while you are there?" I asked her in a lonely voice. She handed me "dinner," a can of squeeze cheese and a pack of Ritz Crackers, and walked out of the door. It hurt a little to be immediately rejected. No, it hurt a lot! I knew I would disappoint her eventually, but thought I at least deserved a chance to please her before I was rejected.

I wondered how I came to this place where I knew no one. Is it okay to eat the food in the house? Is it okay to use the phone? The air-conditioning was on and I was cold, but was it ok to get a blanket? I was afraid to do anything.

When Ms. Emily came home that night, I was still sitting in the same place as when she left. I was careful not to touch anything. She never asked me about myself that night. She just walked in, seemingly uncomfortable in her own home. There were a few weeks of awkwardness in the apartment before we had any real conversations.

A few weeks later, Ms. Emily made it a point to introduce me to all the little black girls in the neighborhood. I met everyone in one night. I was sure these friendships were not going to last. I didn't want friends. I wanted to be alone. Life was so much easier that way. At least alone, I had no ties to people. No pain when I left. I hated that part. It never failed. Just as I got comfortable some place, I moved. I was miserable. I didn't want to put on a facade for all of these people. I didn't want to make friends and I was furious that Ms. Emily made me.

After a few months at Ms. Emily's, I started getting along well with people in the neighborhood. I still fought everyday at school, and hardly ever saw my foster mother, so, in my eyes, I was doing well.

One day in class, I threw paper across the room. My teacher told me she would call home. I quickly commented, "Call home, what is that going to do to me?" I knew kids said that, but in reality they were actually afraid of what their parents would do. I, on the other hand, was not afraid at all. In fact, I dared my teachers to call home. I tried my best to get into trouble in every class except English. English for some reason was important to me. I think I liked reading the stories of lives different than mine.

I was a nightmare to my other teachers, horrible in fact. I was the student who would always debate the teachers' points of view, find fault in their directions, and make their lives miserable. I had tantrums everyday; throwing chairs and turning tables over became the norm. I was frequently sent to the principal's office, but was never reprimanded to the point of suspension. I was usually verbally scolded and sent back to class. It wasn't long before I made it a personal goal to see how badly I could behave without getting suspended. I always felt remorseful for the things I did, but remorse was not enough to make me change my behavior.

One day, I went into the cafeteria to eat lunch and was the "butt" (center) of several jokes. I hated that feeling. The children taunted me about how skinny I was. They talked about my ugly, dark skin, and short hair. When everyone found out I didn't have a real family, they really began to tease me. The jokes seemed to hit home for me because they touched on all the things I hated about myself. I wanted to have light skin and long hair. I wanted a mother and a place to call home. I wanted the children to leave me alone.

Almost immediately, resentment grew inside me towards all the people that had the things I wanted. Those people became my personal targets. My plan was to torture them in any way I could. So I did. I teased every child that had things I wanted in life. And every child that ignored my verbal teasing, were tormented physically. I threw things at them and ruined their nice clothes. For me, misery loved company, and I was miserable. I needed someone to experience at least a fraction of my childhood misery, and I would not rest until they did. Life became very intense.

My English class continued to be a safe place. As part of a poetry project, our instructor asked us to write a poem that told the class something about ourselves. While the majority of the other students wrote about their beautiful skin, nice hair, and fashionable clothing, I wrote a poem called, "The Face Starring Back at Me." When it was time to present our poems to the class, I was beyond nervous. I was a wreck. I had listened intently to my peers. They all seemed so happy with life. I went to the front of the class to read my poem. I lowered my head in shame because I knew the words that would come from my mouth. As I read, tranquility came over the class.

The Face Starring Back at Me

I go shopping to look nice so that people will be impressed with me
Funny how I never know what they're gonna see
Because I never look in the mirror
I just hate the face that's starring back at me

People always tell me to be all I can be
Well all I can be has to be more than I can see
Because I never look in the mirror
I just hate the face that's starring back at me

My mother never has said that she loves me
Perhaps because she sees what I would see
If I ever looked in the mirror
I just hate the face that's staring back at me

I look upon the flawless faces of my peers
Of which I have been envious for years
Telling myself that it's within my reach would be a lie
Look in the mirror, hmmm I'd rather die
I just hate the face starring back at me

My features seem so beautiful when described on paper
Dark skin, slender lips, high cheek bones, all thanks to the Maker
I wonder what it would take
To actually look in the mirror one day
And somehow be at peace
With the face that's starring back at me

The silence in the room was deafening. No one spoke, sniffled, coughed, moved, sneezed... nothing. I carefully looked up and saw my instructor with tears in her eyes. As I quickly took my seat, I heard a few whispers. When the bell rang, the teacher asked to see me after class. She asked if there was anything I wanted to talk about. "No," I said, ashamed of what I had written. I shook my head and left before she asked a follow-up question. I felt so stupid, yet so relieved. It was stupid to allow a group of strangers into my very personal thoughts. Yet I was so relieved to have finally gotten it off my chest.

Naturally, my teacher had a few questions. However, instead of asking me, she went to my other teachers and asked them if they had noticed anything that warranted their concerns about me. I soon became the topic of discussion for weeks after that. The teachers and faculty watched everything I did. They listened to every conversation I had. One teacher even attempted to call home and discuss my situation with my foster mother, but Ms. Emily wasn't home. In fact she was rarely home.

One day I received a call from my social worker while at school. I was told that Ms. Emily was going to Raleigh for several days. I was told to pack some clothes and take them to school with me the next day. As it turned out, Ms. Emily went to Raleigh every week, so a routine began. At the beginning of each week, I packed my clothes and took them to school with me. I did that for sometime before I realized how stupid it was. Think about it. I took clothes with me to school twice a week so that I could live in different respite homes while Ms. Emily was out of town. I would prefer that Ms. Emily would just say she didn't want me there anymore. I did not have nice clothes or shoes, so bringing them to school with me was especially humiliating.

I can recall one day as I walked down the school hall with my "faithful, plastic, trash bag" full of clothes. Apparently I was walking too slowly because my social worker grabbed the bag I was carrying to walk ahead of me. As she did that, the bag tore and my filthy clothes were sprawled about the hallway floor. The students laughed upon seeing my undergarments and other dirty clothes in the hall. I was so embarrassed for myself and furious with my social worker! At first, I could not even bring myself to pick them up. Eventually, with tears in my eyes, I got on my hands and knees and collected my clothes with no help from anyone. I cried as my peers kicked my bras and panties down the hall. I made a mental note of who they were so that I could confront them whenever I mustered enough courage to go back to school.

That same day when I went "home," I used the bathroom I noticed there was a little blood in my panties. Surely this couldn't be my menstrual cycle? Not today of all days! I went to inform my foster mother, but she did not care. I asked her what I was supposed to do.

"They don't teach you kids anything!" She laughed and continued talking to one of her friends on the phone. I heard her comment to her friend that I was dumb for not knowing what a period was and that is why she had to take me into her home - this Negro inner-city youth needed her guidance in order to have any type of success in life. What could I do? I just sat there. Who was I going to call? I had no one.

Ms. Emily was right about one thing, I didn't know much about having a period. I did know however, that I needed some sanitary napkins. I went back to her bedroom and asked her if she could take me to the store.

"I have to go. You'll just have to wait until I get home," she said.

"Well, how long will that be?" I asked sadly. My experience taught me to have a plan to take care of myself. If she was going to take too long, then

I planned to go across the street to the convenience store and steal a package for myself. I had never stolen anything before so I had no idea what I was doing. Ms. Emily never answered my question; she just walked out and slammed the door behind her.

I walked across the street, clueless about how to carry out my plan. How was I going to get out of that store with a pack of sanitary napkins? Was I crazy? I had to steal them. I needed them and I had no money. What else was there for me to do? I couldn't just ask for them? Money is needed to get things in this world, and I had none.

My throat started to close up as the store's automatic door opened. I have to admit, I looked more than a little suspicious. I went to the feminine hygiene section and grabbed something that looked like what I needed. I walked to the front of the store.

"Just bolt out the door," I told myself. "Make a run for it." I stood there thinking for a moment. I didn't have it in me. Finally, I walked up to the register with tears in my eyes. "Can I please have these pads sir?" He looked at me with a bit of confusion. I was humiliated, but there was no one in line behind me so I continued. "I am twelve and I live across the street in those apartments. I have no money, but I need this sir. Please will you let me have this?" I said holding the package in my hands.

"Where is your mother?" he asked.

"I don't know sir. I am not crazy. I just need some money to buy these. I will pay you back somehow," I said and prayed he would not ask anymore questions.

"Let me see..." He felt sorry for me. He went to the back shaking his head and got a female manager. As she came to the front of the store, a line was starting to form behind me. I dreaded having to explain this to her with people surrounding me. When she came towards me, the tears began to well up in my eyes and clog my throat. I felt like I would suffocate. My eyes became filled with tears and through the blur of tears I just shook my head never mind and walked out the door. *I should have just run*, I thought.

"Young lady, come here." The female manager stepped outside the door and handed me a plastic bag. "Sweetheart, this is for you." She went on to explain which brand worked best for her and how to decide which ones would work for me. I was so thankful. She was so nice to me. Someone was nice to me that day and it was someone I had never met. It was a strange feeling to ask for help and receive the help I needed. After being humiliated at school and at the store, I felt a moment of relief and I did not have to steal. I went "home" and read the directions on the package. Luckily for me, there were pictures.

So, I got over that hump on my own and did not get into trouble. On days like that, I wished my sister was still with me. I wanted to tell her I had gotten my period. I needed someone to help me understand my body was ready to reproduce now and that sex had major consequences. No one was available to teach me about being a woman when I needed it. Everything I learned at this time came from my immature misinformed friends. Imagine the difficulty I faced as I learned the real facts about womanhood.

A few weeks later I received a call from my sister's social worker. Justice wanted to visit me. I was ecstatic! I had not seen her for a couple of years and so many things had changed. I talked to my foster mother and she agreed to allow my sister to stay for a few days. When Justice arrived, Ms. Emily was a completely different person. She was kind and helpful; she even took my sister shopping for clothes. I was a little jealous. Ms. Emily never took me shopping.

The visit was a little awkward at first. Justice and I quickly realized we no longer knew each other. She was not the same girl that left home. She had become a young lady and I felt so young and immature. I became determined to grow up fast after that visit so Justice wouldn't think of me as a little girl and forget me. I needed her to be a part of my life and I had no idea how to tell her. As we played "catch-up," I noticed Justice seemed more comfortable with herself than I.

My foster mother seemed eager to impress my sister, so I quickly assessed that I could do whatever I wanted. As Ms. Emily napped, I asked if I could have some company to the house. She nodded and said, "whatever, sure." I invited six of my friends over and my sister cooked a meal for us. Justice prepared practically everything in the house.

Ms. Emily awoke around seven that evening and walked into the living room wearing only a night shirt. Naturally, she was livid that her living room was full of teenagers. She yelled for everyone to leave immediately.

Then Ms. Emily turned to me and said, "You are so stupid. Why would have all these children in my house without permission?" I reminded her that I had already received her permission. She did not hear my words. "Get out!" She yelled at the top of her lungs. "I want you to get out of my house now!" After a few more explosive words, she called my social worker and told her that I had to leave immediately. And that was the end of my placement.

The next day as I gathered my possessions, someone knocked on the door. I expected my social worker; but another woman showed up saying she was my new foster parent. All I knew was her name. For some reason I didn't have a good feeling about this lady, although she seemed very nice. She had a long list of acts to follow and I didn't expect her to be any different. Not a single foster parent had cared about me and I would not even let this new one try.

I understood that I needed someone to care. In fact, I wanted her to like me, but I didn't have the energy to be who I thought she needed me to be. Why was this happening to me? I had been in about six or seven different placements (including respite placements) in just a few short years. I was just so tired of moving. Even if the home was horrible, I preferred to stay than work at getting to know someone else all over again.

As my new foster mother, Ms. Diane, and I drove down the street to my new home, I tried to think of something to say to make her believe that I was a nice person. She was not interested in hearing how I behaved in school or how many friends I had. Ms. Diane wanted to see for herself. She asked me all kinds of questions but never forced me to answer. She listened while I spoke and responded gently with love.

Even after a long ride to the other side of town, I didn't like her. Why? She seemed nice and offered me respect. But I wanted nothing that she offered. I refused to let her into my inner circle, the eye of my storm. There was no one there except me and it was calm. I wanted to keep the storm away and maintain calm. I was so tired of opening myself up only to let the hurt enter. I refused to go through that again.

We walked into her place and I saw my new "home." There were already two young foster children living there as well as her biological son. Her home was beautiful. Ms. Diane lived in a more affluent part of town. Her home was a four-bedroom, three-bathroom split-level home. I was thrilled to learn my room was isolated in the finished basement. I had my own bedroom, living area, and bathroom. The laundry room was in the basement as well. I had my own entrance and as much privacy as I ever wanted. Despite all that, I still wanted nothing from her. Living with her meant I had to change schools again. Honestly, I would rather have slept under a bridge than change schools. Sure I did not care for most of my classmates, but the familiar was better than strangers. Even Ms. Emily was looking good to me.

From day one, Ms. Diane always spoke about God. God is awesome. God is this… God is that. She tried to explain the Bible and the role of guidance in my life. I quickly tuned her and her God out. I was not saved and did not want to be. How was I going to commit my life to serving a God that had me going through all of this sorrow? Ms. Diane told me that I was special and that God had a plan for my life. I told her I did not want to serve this God that had caused me to lose my grandmother and my siblings in a matter of years. In fact, all this God-talk made me angry and I started to direct my anger in that direction. I made sure that my heart was so angry and hard that God would leave me alone. I resolved within myself to never allow God into my life.

Ms. Diane did remind me of my grandmother and that was good. Grandmother always said God was the reason for everything whether people gave Him credit or not. Why in the world would God want credit for all the crap that I had endured? The more rebellious I became in my new home, the more my foster mother pointed to the Bible for answers. She was convinced that the Bible could answer everything. She was sure that my pain was because God had a bigger plan for me. No matter how badly I wanted to believe her, something on the inside of me would not allow that to occur.

My thirteenth birthday and summer vacation were right around the corner. Generally, I attended several sports camps for the first few weeks of summer. After camps, I usually spent a week or two in Virginia with my extended family. When the travel was over I then spent the rest of the summer watching television. It wasn't long before my social worker came into my new home and asked for my summer plans. Before I could respond, Ms. Diane mentioned a camp she learned about at church. It was only a week long and was in mountains. I was adamant that I would not go. If Ms. Diane promoted sending me to camp, I knew it had to be one of those Christian camps and I definitely did not want any part of it. I had my summer all planned out. My social worker thought Ms. Diane's idea was awesome, so against my will, I was signed up to attend a "Christian, mountain camp."

It wasn't long before I was packed and leaving for camp. I knew I had to meet new people from a local church and I was not excited. As I pulled up, I noticed the families saying goodbye to their children. The children also had Bibles in their hands and smiles on their faces. I felt so alone and out of place. I didn't have a family… a Bible…or a smile. When it was time to say goodbye to my foster mother, I would not look in her direction. I was still upset about being forced to attend this camp. I wanted to sit alone on the bus, but the children were so friendly, they talked to me and refused to leave me alone. I decided this was not the best place to curse at anyone, so I just sat quietly and tried to ignore them. I didn't want to be mean to anyone, but I didn't want these new girls in my face either. I made small talk. It worked pretty well. I learned that if I initiated a conversation then the girls were less likely to bother me. I thought about basketball camp as the bus drove us to the mountains. "Just get through this week and the summer was all mine," I said to myself.

We arrived at our cabins late that afternoon. Upon receiving our cabin assignments, each cabin was instructed to present a piece of scripture to the entire group before dinner. It was not difficult to decide which scripture because I only knew one that my grandmother taught me. So whatever the girls in my cabin decided, we would use.

As the groups made their presentations, I was noticeably uncomfortable. I shifted in my seat and I wanted to go home. Everyone was so happy to make their presentation. I was so angry, felt stupid and out of place. My mind wandered. It seemed that since entering foster care, I always felt stupid and out of place. I wanted to feel comfortable like Justice did on our visit. After dinner, one of the camp staff gave Bibles to anyone without one and asked that we bring it to all of our events. Well, it seemed I was now an official camper.

The next day a Caucasian man sang a song. This was the first time I actually paid attention. The man closed his eyes as he sang. The music seemed to touch his heart. It touched mine too. I always liked music. It helped me find peace when everything around me seemed chaotic. This music was very peaceful. I liked it. I looked around and saw many other young girls were also touched by the music. I decided to listen more attentively to the words. Obviously it was a Christian song, but I liked it.

I sat alone in my cabin that night and tried to recall the words to the song but I couldn't. I tried to fall asleep, but I was very restless. I lay in bed the rest of the night and looked at the ceiling. Before I knew it, the sun had risen and I had not slept at all.

During breakfast I watched the girls eat and talk with one another. Most of the girls already knew each other so they were comfortable. I was the "odd girl out" at camp. I was alone in many respects: I knew no one personally, only one girl there looked like me, I was the only one who didn't want to be there, and I was the only foster child.

The assignment that day was to make a presentation about what we learned the previous day. The only thing I could remember was the praise and worship songs. The songs were the only thing I liked. Fortunately, music was part of every session.

During the after breakfast session, tears came to my eyes and my heart began to beat rapidly during the music. I wanted to be filled with happiness. I was desperate to be happy with life. At that point I did not have a single ounce of joy in my life but decided to open myself to whatever the joy and hope the world could offer. I decided I deserved some happiness just like the other campers, and needed to change myself to make it happen.

I skipped dinner that night and went straight to my room. While the other girls were in the dinning hall, I lay across my bed looked at the ceiling. I tried to recall the lyrics to all the songs, and reason why I wanted to be happy. I sat alone in my cabin and recalled my sorrow, the ways I hurt people, and how I had hurt myself. I apologized to God and decided to believe in a better life. I resolved to change my behavior and find hope in the people and things that were in my life. I decided to not allow anger to rule my world. This was the very first time I remembered feeling at peace. I felt the hope that my brother offered many years ago. I felt faith in my sister; Justice found me and wanted to see me. I felt relief that Ms. Diane didn't leave me the many times I rejected her. I still didn't know where I was headed, but I was no longer willing to be angry for the sake of being angry.

Being in the eye of a storm is a paradox. While the term suggests that you are in the middle of chaos and challenges, you are not. The eye of the storm is, in fact, the safest place to be. It is calm and protected… like the eyeball. It is the place where clarity lies despite total pandemonium surrounding it.

I saw myself in this place for the first time. I was in a place of peace and clearly seeing what I had done to myself and others through my anger. I decided it was time to venture out and expand my inner circle with my new vision of hope and determination to conquer the turmoil around me.

CHAPTER 5

the Aftermath

People often seek relief when the core of the storm has passed their lives. However, I find that people often have the most difficulty with life after the major hardships have somewhat subsided; not during life's sufferings as one might think. I've heard people question why they ever had to endure such life-changing trials in the first place. During the struggle, they do what is required to survive, and then question what they did to deserve those things in the first place.

I am reminded of a quote that reads, "The pain of my suffering brings forth the gold of godliness." This means that things I have to endure help shape my character; that what I am able to bear helps me build my resiliencies; and that my ability to sustain trials shows my strength and exactly where my faith lies.

While the aftermath of a storm brings calm it can also be more detrimental than the actual storm itself. Why? *Because, while in the midst of a storm nothing is hidden,* and you can see what is going on and can prepare for the inevitable. The aftermath, on the other hand is less predictable. You are confident the storm's worst is past and therefore you put your umbrella away and let your guard down. While it is probably true that you endured the worst, the aftermath is unknown. It is like living in an area prone to tornados. The forecast predicts one on the way; so you prepare. You go to the store, stock up your cellar, and weatherproof your home. As the tornado clears, the boards come off the windows. Then a second, less ferocious and yet unexpected wind begins to blow, destroying everything you have worked so hard to preserve. That was the case in my life. I was more infuriated about the aftermath than the actual storm.

I learned through my church community and faith that suffering can build perseverance, character, and ultimately hope. I struggled with this teaching, but found it was true for me. I found my increased hope did not disappoint me; it helped build my faith for a better future. With my hope came increased resiliency. I became strong and determined inside to do positive things for myself. I was always a strong and determined person, but had used that to fuel my anger. Life was going to be different… it needed to be different. It was this belief, my hope and faith that helped me through the aftermath.

My new foster mother, Ms. Diane, was beginning to grow on me. I still did not hug or tell her I loved her, but I liked her. It was a start. She was still a little too overwhelming when she spoke about God. I did not tell her that I had asked God for forgiveness and to enter my heart when I had returned home. I eventually told the girls in my cabin, but I waited to tell Ms. Diane because I didn't want her to make a big deal about it. I wanted her to be pleased that I enjoyed the camp and that was it. Ms. Diane noticed an immediate change in my behavior. I was more polite. I was interested in school and I wanted to go to youth group at church. There were still a few things that I did not want to change.

I wanted to wear my jeans to church and still had a problem with my language. I used more profanity than most people. Profanity got my point across and instilled fear in the hearts of the people around me and I loved that. I did give up my "pre-camp" music. I made a conscious decision to listen to Christian music. It was a little weird at first, but not at all difficult to do. I simply prayed that the desire for my previous music would go away.

There was still a lot of work to clean up my act, but I was on my way. Aside from the occasional blow up, I did well managing my anger. I almost loved life. As much as I hated to admit it, I started to love my new foster mother. I entered high school with optimism I had never had. Hope and faith were building inside me.

Beginning to love Ms. Diane was a big deal. Usually I refused to let people get too close to me for fear I would become too attached. It seemed that just as I became comfortable with people in my life, I would receive a horrible "curve ball," something totally unexpected would happen. I hoped this time would be different, but I had to do more than hope. I became angry with myself every time I did something that disappointed Ms. Diane, which happened much too frequently. She was all I had and I could not afford to loose her. I did not get along with the other children in the neighborhood nor did I get along with my new social worker - Ms. Diane was the only person who accepted me. Although I wanted to accept her, I was so afraid of that "curve ball."

One evening my social worker came over for a home visit. Everything was going pretty well before she came. We sat and talked about my academic and athletic plans for the upcoming school year. Nothing she said bothered me at first; until she mentioned how my lack of affection and appreciation were serious character flaws needing to be immediately addressed. She demanded that I hug my foster mother and let her know I appreciated her. I can't really recall which of her outlandish suggestions sent me over the top. I tried to explain I was not the hugging type, but that was no longer a good excuse.

In my mind I had come a long way. I was furious that this woman, whom I barely knew, sought to coerce me to show physical affection to anyone! Respectful behavior was a new high for me and a first step. Who was this social worker to demand more of me? Sure Ms. Diane was worthy of a hug, but if the truth be told, I was still afraid. If I loved openly, I would risk exposure and thereby be vulnerable to rejection. I knew that and decided to keep my distance. The more my social worker talked about it, the more furious I became. So, I did what I always did when faced with an uneasy decision - I left. I went to my room and avoided the situation. It was not so much my social worker I was trying to avoid as it was my foster mother's feelings. I did not want Ms. Diane to feel that her unmistakable love for me was in vain. I just was not ready to show it yet! My love for her did not lack depth; however, I had yet to arrive to a place where I could let it be transparent.

I walked down the stairs into my bedroom. I sat on the bed yelling for my social worker not to come into my room. She obviously was not listening or she didn't care. "Get out!" I screamed. She didn't listen. I looked around intently for something to hurl at her. I reached for the closest shoe. I threw the boot at her as hard as I could. It missed her by inches, but it hit the huge mirror over the dresser. The mirror was gigantic. When the shoe hit it the mirror, it fell forward and shattered into pieces. There was no repairing it. I was shocked. I had not intended to break it. I just wanted that woman out of my room.

I looked at my foster mother who stood in the doorway. She looked more hurt than angry. I overheard her telling my social worker that she owned that mirror for more than twenty years. I felt so stupid that I allowed my anger to get the best of me yet again. I was sure Ms. Diane wanted me to leave so I decided to get a jump start. I packed some clothes into a book bag and ducked out the door when they weren't looking.

As I was walking up the street, I had no idea of where I was going. I thought of all the things I lost because of my temper. I didn't want to leave, but if I had to, I would leave on my own terms. I sat on the curb a few blocks from the house contemplating my next move. Before I knew it, hours had past and so had the county car. The social worker actually drove past several times. I even saw a police car.

I knew how to run away; what to expect, the procedures, and wasn't scared. In fact, running away was typical behavior for me. I was different from the other kids I knew in foster care because they generally "ran" when they didn't want to comply with the rules of the house. I, on the other hand, ran when I knew that a move was on the way. I was hardly ever caught because I generally went back on my own. It's not that I couldn't make it on my own, but I often just got tired of "couch-surfing."

So, what was my plan? I started to think. I knew I would miss my foster mother too much if I stayed away. She seemed to care about me. That was huge. I thought about some of the other foster parents and was convinced that if I stayed away from Ms. Diane, I may never find someone who cared so much. Truthfully, I have had some of the worst foster parents in the world, but also some of the best! I tried to draw a correlation between my childhood and the foster parents that I have had. I determined that the best parents built my character and faith, and the worse fed my internal turmoil. You see, being in foster care can come with as many transitions in and outside the home as well as in and outside yourself.

Most foster children are not fortunate enough to remain in the same home for their entire stay in foster care. Therefore, numerous changes in living arrangements and school assignments become commonplace, at least they did for me. All of the changes allowed me to constantly reinvent myself. While there were certain constants in my personality, such as I would not take crap from anyone, most of the quirks I did not like about myself could be transformed when I moved to another place. I was able to change my grades, my friends, and most importantly my looks. I was able to recreate everything about me as I pleased. If I was unpopular, I could become popular. If I had short hair, I could grow it longer. If I had poor grades, I could get straight A's. Life was great once I got use to the system and learned how to be a chameleon. I changed with the environment. In a sense, this made me feel very powerful, but very unstable. Most children in care go through identity crises because they have been separated from their families. There is another element of an identity crisis when someone is constantly moved from place to place; this continuous state of transition produces a false sense of reality in many foster children.

This was the first time I really wanted to stay in the same place. I had to go back and apologize, but that would be a real blow to my pride. I sat on the curb until the sun set. I was still unsure of what to do. I was a little sleepy and I began to fall asleep right there on the street. I started walking home and thought of how I would get around an apology. When I walked into the house everyone was still there; the police, my social worker, and my foster mother. My social worker demanded I apologize for all the trouble I created. She shouted at me for being so ungrateful. My foster mother glanced at me and then back to my social worker and said, "That's ok, she looks tired." It was as if she knew what I felt. I really was sorry for my tantrum. I was grateful for her and my pride was still in tact.

I had been with Ms. Diane more than a year and things were wonderful. My grades were not the best, just average, and I still fought all the time in school, but I was happy at home. I was almost fifteen and about to enter my sophomore year in high school. During the summer I went home to Virginia, as usual. When I returned to my foster home, I discovered Ms. Diane moved. I did not change parents, just homes. I understood the changes were short-term but little did any of us know they would last awhile. Ms. Diane fell on hard times and I had no idea. We lost a beautiful home, but I was still happy. I had her, and I still had my own room.

I knew DSS was not going to be pleased that we lost our home. I still hoped I did not have to leave Ms. Diane. She was my entire world. I had gotten to know her family and several of them even knew me by name. This was a very big deal for me considering I was quite a loner. I did not let anyone in and there she was. She stole my heart. One day, I even hugged her, said "I love you," and meant it! I would do anything to stay with her forever. I learned the system very well. I knew there was someone I could talk to in an attempt to buy a little more time with her. I did just that. We fought hard to stay together. We lived with her parents and with other people as needed.

The more moves we made, the more often I changed schools. I didn't care though. I was still happy at home with Ms. Diane. I was dealt a huge blow while we lived with a friend of hers. I learned Ms. Diane was no longer my foster parent. I was not upset at my new foster mother; I was upset that no one told me. Here I thought she was still my foster mother and she didn't even have the decency to tell me. In hindsight, I understand that she did not want to hurt me. The truth would have been better.

After the license was switched, she left to stay with her parents for awhile. Ms. Diane called to tell me she would call and come by whenever I wanted, but she would not live with me. I was so hurt. We still attended the same church so I saw her every week for the most part, but I was still distraught. That is one thing I hated most about foster care. Just as I allowed someone to love me, I had to leave them, and it did not matter for what reason. I felt they (DSS) could have worked with us. It was not Ms. Diane's fault that we lost our house, but I thought that when they saw how much I loved Ms. Diane, DSS would work to keep us together.

I guess love is not enough. I suppose for DSS, stability is more important than love. Why can't I have both? Other kids get both! I had been so used to moving that the transitions I made in this foster home did not bother me. DSS had me moving from school to school and home to home anyway, so why couldn't I continue to do that to stay with my foster mother? I guess that's one of the things I'll never understand. For the record, if given the choice between stability and lasting love, I would choose love in a heartbeat. Love for me in its richest form, offers stability that DSS could never provide, no matter how hard they tried.

My new foster mother, Ms. Smith, could do nothing to make me feel welcomed. I rejected everything. I made up my mind that no one would get close to me ever again. I took a step back in my personal development and lost both faith and hope. I fell into a pit of confusion and despair. I was not ready to start all over. I did not have the energy. I was not ready for a new school or new rules. Life stunk! Everything was going well. Why did this have to happen?

It was time to make some decisions for myself. I needed to feel as if I was in control of my own destiny. Ms. Smith wasn't "bad," so why was I so unhappy? I had changed so many schools that I had run out of identities to assume. I was so depressed that I went many days without speaking a single word at school. When the teachers asked me direct questions, I just shrugged my shoulders and put my head on the desk, regardless of whether I knew the correct answer or not. I detested my peers and dared any of them to cross me. No one would ever take me as a weakling! No way! I needed to be mean whether I wanted to or not. That was my armor.

Usually, after I transitioned to a new home I would reevaluate my personality quirks. Then I would change them before I arrived at my new school. But I had now exhausted my range of personalities. People would say, "Just be yourself," but who was that? I had become so accustomed to altering my identity to suit my new environment that I wasn't sure who I was anymore. Did I want long hair or short? Was I still into baggy clothes or had I become more womanly and wanted to show off my body? Was I scholarly or stupid? Did I want a boyfriend who was a gentleman or a bad boy? I was at a crossroads.

I was not sure who I was or wanted to be, nor did I have the energy to become someone else. Besides, the school year was coming to a close, and it seemed pointless to expend more energy on a time-limited problem. My plan was to suffer through the remainder of my junior year and hope the summer would bring happiness. If all else failed, I could always work myself to death.

The summer was just unbearable. I was stuck in the house so much that I decided to work three jobs just so I would not have to go home. I worked for as many hours as I could, but I had to go home sometime. Ms. Smith and I did not get along. The other foster children in the house were okay, but most of them were too young to understand what was going on in my head. *I was too young to understand.* The summer before my senior year should have been amazing. After all, I was only months away from exiting the foster care system. A social worker came to me over the summer and asked me to think about staying in foster care until I was twenty-one. "Are you serious? You've got to be kidding?" I thought. I would not stay in foster care one day past my eighteenth birthday and would leave sooner if I could! My only thought of happiness came from imagining my freedom from DSS. Luckily for them, that decision was a little bit down the road. I was coming upon my seventeenth birthday and I knew it would be a disappointment. They all were.

One day just before my birthday, Ms. Smith and I had a big argument about why I was so close to my mentors and not with her family. She said I was ungrateful. She said I would never know what its like to belong to a real family. She said it as if she was declaring some major epiphany. I already knew that. It was not that I did not want to have a family; it's just that I wanted to *choose* my family. I dreamed that some family and I would want each other at the same time. Ms. Smith and I argued for a while before I came to realize she was never going to understand my perspective. One major turnoff was that she offered her family to me as if she was offering me the most precious diamond on earth. When I refused to even admire her "diamond," she made me feel stupid. After all, who would pass up the opportunity to keep a precious diamond for themselves? My attitude had nothing to do with her family. They were cool people. I just wanted my own diamond. Every time Ms. Smith talked about family, it ended in an argument between us. She would get upset if I wanted to spend time with my mentor because I never wanted to spend time with her family or anyone else for that matter. I knew I could not go through this for another whole year.

Finally, I confided in my mentor. I told her I was totally and genuinely unfulfilled and depressed. I did not want to be there anymore. I decided that it was time to run and this time I was never going back. It was either that or suicide. I sure hated life, but I was not sure that I was ready to end mine. That's a pretty permanent solution to what may be a temporary problem. I despised the foster care system for what (I perceived) it had done to me. I had to leave now or I would never make it out. If I left now, whatever hardships I faced would at least be caused by my own doing and not the result of what someone or something did to me (usually without my consent). I packed my bags and just before I headed out into the real world I called my mentor to say goodbye. "Don't do anything until tomorrow," she said. The next day she offered me a place to live. Was she serious? I ignored her the first time. The next day I asked if she was serious and thank God she was.

I made the decision to accept my mentor's offer. I was so thrilled! I had "hope" again. Although I ignored her offer at first, I decided to go. I can recall the day that she was granted emergency custody. I was working at a fast food joint when I received a call from "Lorraine." I could hear the excitement in her voice. "Are you ready to come home?" It was like a fairytale. My heart leapt with excitement. Was it true? Was I really going *home*? Over the years, "home" had taken on so many different meanings.

It was a little more than two weeks after my birthday and I was making another transition. This brought the tally to over a dozen homes and multiple schools. In fact, the school I enrolled in my senior year was the same school I attended my freshman year. Isn't it funny how life can sometimes bring a person full circle?

Prior to Lorraine's call, I had been having a horrible day at work, not to mention the argument with Ms. Smith prior to leaving for work. She had been upset with me for "going behind her back" and talking to my Guardian Ad Litem about my desire to move without first mentioning it to her. Maybe she was right? Perhaps I should have spoken with her first. Given our tumultuous history, I decided against it. The other reason I did not tell her was that her daughter, son-in-law, and grandkids were visiting from New York. I did not think it was a good idea to bring it up while she had a house full of people. I guess that's part of being a teenager. Sometimes you make bad decisions.

I have a feeling that no matter how or when I said I wanted to move, it would not have ended well. Walking home from work that day, I was excited because I was moving out. I had already started packing earlier in the week when my social worker told me there was a good possibility that Lorraine's home would work out. As I approached the house, I saw all of my belongings thrown into boxes on the porch. There was no order to anything. Imagine how low I felt to see all of my things haphazardly thrown into boxes with no regard to their value. I was furious! Ms. Smith said whatever I did not get in one trip it would be thrown away. So when Lorraine arrived in her small, two-door Mitsubishi Eclipse I panicked; yet was relieved at the same time. Panicked because I was certain that all my things were not going to fit into her sports car; and relieved that this hellish nightmare was about to end. I mentally decided what things I could leave behind just in case. I packed the necessities in her car first. Luckily everything fit and I said goodbye with a sigh of relief. I was determined to go into my new home and enter my senior year with optimism no matter how much I felt like Ms. Smith was trying to ruin it for me.

It took nine days from my decision to accept Lorraine's offer to actually move to her home. There was still an adjustment period but overall, it was delightful. I had to get used to her love for me. At first, it was difficult to tell her thank you and "I love you," but that period didn't last as long. This time was different because I made the decision to move. Life was great again. I played sports. My grades were awesome. I had awesome friends and, not to mention, a very handsome, Christian boyfriend. There was no need to search for a new identity anymore because "Mommy" (I now called Lorraine by this name) began to teach me who I was on the "inside." One of the best parts of life was that I still attended the church Ms. Diane introduced me to, which meant I saw her regularly. I also had an open invitation to stop by her home whenever I wanted. Mommy made sure that I maintained contact with Ms. Diane by taking me to her home as often as possible. Mommy even tried to bridge the gap between my biological siblings and me. She made arrangements for my big sister and niece to visit us. It was like all the pieces of my past and current lives were coming together.

About a year or so after what I named "the best move of my life," I received another crushing blow. Ms. Diane called to say that she was sick. She was diagnosed with cancer and given six to eight months to live. I never even expected it. I should have seen it coming because life was just going too smoothly. My world was crushed. I could not imagine living without her, yet here I was. We tried to spend a lot of time together, but that was even too much at times. I watched her become frail and fragile – almost wasting away – yet she was still a very content person. She never complained even while in hospice (a service to help people die with dignity). Sometimes she said she was cold; beyond that she was so pleasant in her obvious discomfort.

It was almost Ms. Diane's birthday and I heard a few people were going by the hospital to have a birthday celebration. I was stuck working at the fast food restaurant but decided to go over on my break. The hospital was only a few miles up the road so I could do that rather quickly. Come break time, the restaurant was slammed packed and I was not permitted to leave. So I decided to call and at least say hello. Ms. Diane sounded so weak on the phone; I had to see her.

All of a sudden I felt panicked. There was a new urgency growing within me to hug and see her. Memories of Grandma flooded my mind. I didn't want anything to take me by surprise the way it had with Grandma so many years ago. How was I going to get out of work? Mommy came by the restaurant about thirty minutes after I spoke to Ms. Diane. She spoke with the manager on duty and told me to come with her. We went to the hospital to see Ms. Diane; this woman who had given so much to me. I was overwhelmed with the melancholy atmosphere. Everyone seemed so down and depressed. I looked into Ms. Diane's eyes and told her I loved her. I apologized for any sadness I caused. I thanked her for taking a chance on me. At that moment, it seemed as if we were the only two people in the room, although many people had come to celebrate Ms. Diane's birthday. I gazed into her eyes as she escaped to a better place; a place with no sickness; a place of joy. I looked at her and knew I would have given my life for her to feel no pain.

Ms. Diane had passed away. There was a void left after her death. I was so traumatized that I barely spoke to anyone for days. I cried uncontrollably for a while, and then reality set in. She was really gone. I had to find a way to numb the pain. I became totally consumed with work. I worked three jobs, went to school full time, and played sports. I worked all day most days. I was not an enjoyable person to be around. I was gloomy and despondent and my attitude was always so oppressed. I did not eat and could not sleep. On top of this, I got the flu. I knew I had to get well but my only focus was Ms. Diane as we prepared to lay her to rest. My thoughts were consumed with memories of her. She was responsible for loving me out of my shell. I am living proof of her belief that love can cover a multitude of sins.

Mommy was so compassionate during this time. She never forced me to "talk." She waited for me to let go and cry. I just could not let go. I was afraid that if I started to cry, I might never stop. It was times like this that I wished I had never made my heart open to love. While being loved is wonderful, the absence of that love can be devastating. I soon realized Ms. Diane and I had to be separated some years ago. What if I had been living with her at the time of her death? I would have really lost my mind! I believed this was divine intervention. In my mind, God was really looking out for me. He knew exactly what I needed before I knew. Even with that epiphany, I was still so angry. In some ways I felt like I was learning how to accept the good and bad things that were happening in my life and starting to see that some of the bad things resulted in building my faith.

There were some things I wanted to say at the funeral, but I didn't have the courage. If I could do it all over again, I would say what was in my heart at the time:

My Dearest Diane

You comforted me in my time of need
You introduced me to the peace
That only in Christ could be

You offered me love
That at first I threw away
Now that you're gone
I'm begging you to stay
You said don't cry for you
Because death is what this life is about
You told me of a better place you could go
By invitation because you had no doubt
You said He'd look up your name
In this Lamb's Book of Life
You said you looked forward
To a life in the absence of strife
You taught me to be strong
And to hold my head up high
You taught me that if I called Him,
God would draw nigh
One thing you forgot to teach me
Now that you've left me here
Is how to deal with loosing you
Yet still hold you so dear
I am a woman now
And I understand full well
That your leaving here was to reap the rewards
Of life beyond the veil
I wish you would have told me
That it would hurt this much
I wish I was prepared
For the absence of your touch
I am still hurting
But I celebrate for you
For I know that everything you said
About our God is true
Inasmuch as it pains me

For us to be apart
I am solely relying on Him
To heal my broken heart
So hats off to you
My Dearest Diane
For you get to adorn
That beautiful wedding band
For after enduring this life
So sure and so steady
I'm glad the wedding of the Lamb has come
And His bride hath made herself ready

~ To the late Delbra Diane Alston

I always tell people that I have had the absolute best foster parents and the absolute worse. People like Ms. Diane do not come into this world often; I am glad that I had the chance to know and love her. She blessed my life and now it was time for her to rest in peace.

Different stages of the storm taught me important lessons about life and survival. My grandmother used to tell me that God would be with me no matter what. It was not until much later in life that I started to understand her. I've learned that it takes faith and hope to survive situations like I've experienced. Each person has to determine where they get that faith and hope. My Grandmother and some foster parents helped me gain this through Christianity. Other people may find it through various forms of faith, a special person, or internal belief in "who" they are. Wherever it begins, a network of caring people needs to help build and nurture it. Negative people will work against it.

Surviving the storm takes many positive forces and I was just beginning to believe those forces were operating in my life. At this point, I believed the major part of the storm had ended. There was still a lot to learn, but at least the storm was over.

CHAPTER 6

the Storm is over?

A friend told me a story of riding in the car with his mother when he first got his driver's license. There was a severe thunderstorm out. It was a blinding rain where the visibility was less than a mile. All of the other cars decided to pull over underneath the bridge and wait for the storm to pass. My friend's mother told him, "Son, look, everyone else has pulled over; I think we should pull over too and wait for the storm to pass." My friend said to his mother, "Why should we wait? If we keep driving, we will eventually make it to the other side of the storm."

I learned a powerful lesson that day. There are options that can determine how we handle the storms. Sometimes the safest thing is to pull over and allow the storm to pass over you. On the other hand, sometimes the most prudent thing is to keep driving because eventually, "we will make to the other side of the storm." I wonder how many people pulled over that day. How long did they sit there? Were they late for appointments or missed important people while they waited for the storm to pass?

Imagine how many foster youth play it safe by pulling over and letting life's storms pass over them? Most youths are never encouraged to take responsibility for their lives until it is nearly too late. Social workers and other adults make many decisions for them and youths think, "What's the use in trying?" Therefore some youths are overwhelmed by their situation and allow the "downpours" of life to throw them off course. Then when it's time to leave foster care; youths can be so unprepared to handle the world. It's difficult to know what to do and where to start. That was me. I was so confused in the beginning and when things began to calm down; I believed my storm was over. Maybe the real answer was I chose a different option to handle my storm? Maybe I chose to face my storm with hope and assume some responsibility to calm it.

Just before moving in with Lorraine, I had been through a lot and was feeling hurt. It was very painful. I allowed myself to wallow in self-pity and began another journey in self-doubt. It was exhausting, and I wanted to give up fighting for a good life.

Have you noticed that just before I give up and loose faith, something changes? I had started to think that I would never get a "real" mother and just before I gave up, Lorraine was there to care for me. I thought it was interesting that Lorraine had been in my life for so long but not as a "mother."

I met Lorraine at a local church I had attended for a number of years. She quickly became my mentor and a dear friend. She and I spoke nearly every day. It was important to me to have someone to talk to outside of my foster home. I found it helpful to open up and trust someone I did not live with – that way; they could not ask me to leave.

My foster home, at the time I met Lorraine, was okay but it was not a great fit for me. For starters, I was the oldest youth in my foster home so I had no one "like me." As days went by in that home, I became more and more rebellious. I hated living there. I decided to get a job after school so that I did not have to be home all the time. It worked for a while. I would come home, pretend to do homework, call Lorraine, and then I was off to work. This system worked for months. It made living in foster care almost tolerable. My foster mother was not a bad person; I just needed a home that was a better fit for my needs, wants, and goals.

The night I decided to run away is when I called Lorraine. This is how I knew I loved her; she was the only person I wanted to call and say goodbye. I could not imagine my life without her and knew that when I ran, I would not see her anymore. My relationship with her was the only obstacle. Her response to me that night changed my life forever. I'm glad I promised her to stick around for another day.

When Lorraine asked me to come live with her, I realized that she loved me as much as I loved her. I had not experienced real love since I lived with Ms. Diane. I also remember feeling excitement and fear all at once. What if Lorraine was not serious and I said yes? I would look like an idiot. Fortunately, she was serious and I learned to trust my instincts.

I moved in with Lorraine on August 3, 1999. It was such an exciting day! I remember the goose bumps and anxiety filling my stomach. I could not wait for her to arrive. I made sure I was busy all day so the day would move quickly. I had the feeling of knowing exactly what I wanted and being absolutely certain I would get it. That confidence made me certain that when I got what I wanted, it would be great. I knew from the moment I moved in with Lorraine that she would be everything I wanted in a mother. I was sure of it. She was awesome.

When Lorraine finally arrived, I felt like a kid who had gone to bed early on Christmas Eve prepared to wake up for the excitement of Christmas morning and some wonderful gifts. As we packed the car, I tried to contain my excitement. I suspect she could tell anyway. I looked forward to the "honeymoon period" with my new "Mommy," when everything would be amazing. I knew she eventually would have to show me who was boss. Living with Mommy was everything I ever wanted and more. She changed my life and I am grateful. I must say, it was worth the wait.

As I look back on this time, I have come to believe that had I been given a mother as soon as my heart desired, I would not have fully appreciated her role in my life. I would not have been mature enough to treat her as a person of tremendous value. I treated some of my other foster parents horribly so I understand now why some of them asked me to leave. My experiences with foster parents taught me a lot about respect, authority, love, and how different people and situations are.

Foster care has taught me to avoid "pity parties" as a response to my situation. I understand that it is important to be tough in foster care and that much is learned though both the good and bad moments. I decided to use my experiences to teach other foster youths that it is possible to be happy while in foster care, even with the dark days. I am still a little too "emotionally" hard and fear letting my armor come off completely sometimes. I hardly ever allow anyone new into my inner circle. It's how I protect myself and its okay to find a way to keep negativity out. However, sometimes, it's a bad thing, because I may miss out on some amazing relationships or opportunities that could help meet my goals.

It was not hard to let Mommy into my circle because I knew she truly loved me. Her behavior was consistently about love. It also helped that I had known her for awhile. One day Mommy taught me a new lesson about love that I'll never forget. She said, "Sweetie, you cannot control how much I love you by anything you do because it is my decision, not yours." This wrecked everything I had ever learned about love. She spoke about love as a personal decision not based on the others' behavior. Mommy's behavior to me was always based on love because she made that personal decision, and it was not based on my behavior. I always thought that love had to be reciprocated, but now, I know differently. The true measure of love is in its ability to remain despite resistance.

The irony in this storm is that from the very beginning, I was slated to successfully make it to the end; all I had to do was wait it out and successfully live through it. I spent so much energy fighting my way through the storm, oftentimes creating more damage. I did learn to build trust with a few people and find faith in a better day. I never did loose my dream to find a family that I chose.

I remember my older sister saying, "You are a 'Charles.' We do get beat up, but we don't loose." I was glad to be a "Charles" because I could fight on the back of that established reputation. In fact, my opponents knew the power I had before I ever did. My goal was not to hit hard; it was to avoid getting hit. I learned it takes double the energy to throw a punch and miss than it does to land the punch the first time. So I was clever and avoided contact. Contact could be defined as both physical and emotional. I avoided both.

After every fight, the fighter has to go through a period of restoration to heal and rebuild. Although a fighter continues to train, the restoration period is less intense and involves the help of several people. These people (such as coaches, family, friends, physician, etc.) all have the same goal, to heal the fighter. The same is true at the conclusion of a storm. There has to be a clean-up period and it too requires the help of people, positive people with a similar goal… to heal.

CHAPTER 7

disaster Relief

Generally after a huge storm is over, the victims, or those that were adversely affected by the storm require help rebuilding their lives. The victims often allow help from others in order to relieve some of the stress. This is called disaster relief. Each part of my storm was meant to refine and define me. I really believe my storm helped make a better me.

Consider the work of a potter. Before the potter creates a ceramic object, he has to decide what he wants to make. He needs a vision. Then he places the heap of clay onto the wheel and goes to work shaping his intended dish. While the clay is still pliable he is able to shape it into the object he desires. After his piece has taken form, he evaluates its usefulness and appeal. If the object is a bowl, is it large enough for its designed purpose? Is it durable enough to withstand the extremities of heat and cold? The potter then places it in a kiln of fire once it meets approval. The kiln is designed to give the object a high gloss finish and solid form. The object is then placed in a dark room to cool down before it can be used. Once fired in the kiln, the piece of clay is much more difficult to reshape. In order to redesign a piece of clay that has been hardened by the inferno, it must be broken and re-purposed, repeating the process as often as necessary.

Hardships are often defined as "going through the fire." It may help to consider hardships as teaching experiences which "shape" lives. So in truth, although hardships feel as if you are "going through fire," they can be viewed as "wheel" moments - still in the shaping and formation stage. The fire is a privilege. The "kiln" period suggests that you, the completed work of clay, are finished and have satisfied your purpose. In fact, this moment can often bring clarity and understanding of why the hardships were necessary.

It is no different from being in the storm; the toughest times of your storm can be compared to the ever changing moments on the "wheel." When all is said and done, the "fire" will refine all those characteristics and experiences. The fire will make you practice the things you learned while on the wheel, despite your resistance. Finishing this clay-making process, or in my case foster care, is a great thing. It means I survived, but it also means I thrived. I did not sit idling by. I learned some things while on the wheel and have taken those experiences as part of me into adulthood.

I knew that life after foster care was going to be challenge. I had become accustomed to life as a nomad in the foster care system. My home was nowhere and everywhere. Now I had to get use to stability. I wasn't even sure I knew what stability was. I did know that part of it included living in one place. There was no longer the threat of being kicked out. No more excitement, running away, drama. Would this be boring? This was a family. I tried to remember the days living with my grandparents, brothers, and sisters. It seemed so long ago. The days were predictable. The adults were predictable. I knew they loved me. Stability.

Curfews, chores, study sessions, and rules. It was all starting to be a bit overwhelming. How could I allow this woman to come into my world and teach all these things? I had passed the hard part - trusting her. I knew she could be trusted. Did I really have to obey her? One thing is for sure, she believed I could be successful and somehow she made me believe it too. I started thinking about life beyond foster care and all of the possibilities. I wondered about college and if it was an option for me. Can you believe that? I asked questions about college. No one, not a single person, in my family ever attended college. Who was I to think it was an option for me? I came from the same place they had. I grew up in that same neighborhood and went to some of the same schools. Who was I to think I had a real chance in college?

I had a lot to learn and only a short time to learn it. Mommy seemed to know exactly where to start. She started with the obvious; I had to submit to authority. I had to understand the difference between me and someone "in charge" and respect it. I knew this would be a challenge. When other people (including those with authority) told me what to do, I never listened. Now, I had to enter a new phase. When I arrived at my new home, Mommy and I discussed her expectations. She made certain that I understood this was no longer her home - it was "our" home.

She said, "I am not asking you to come and stay here. I am asking that you live here. If you ever leave it will be because you decided to leave. I am in this thing for a lifetime."

She was so sincere and I had no idea how to respond. She was no longer my mentor. She was my mother now. Was I ready for this? A few days after I moved into her home, I was given a curfew. I never had a curfew... ever. Here, at seventeen, on the brink of my senior year in high school, and now I have a curfew? Can you believe that? There was a first time for everything, and I suppose that included a curfew. It shocked me at first but really didn't bother me too much because I wasn't interested in hanging out. I did pretty well meeting the curfew. It was a few weeks or so before I missed it – and even then, it wasn't my fault. Really it wasn't.

There were other pressing issues to manage and those were not as superficial as having to adopt a curfew. Many years prior, I committed myself to adopt a more positive attitude and decided it was time to work on it. I found support in my Christian family and at church but I had an angry, volatile past to resolve.

The year prior to my move I still fought in school and disrespected my teachers. I was such a loner. I never bothered anyone unless they bothered me. When others did bother me I never let it get too far. I just hit them in the face a few times and life was good again. It only took a few examples before people got the message and left me alone. My plan was to stop being so violent - so instead of fighting, I had to learn to articulate my problems. This was going to be difficult. While in foster care, I learned to act out my feelings. It seemed everyone expected it. Acting out worked fine because foster care gave me the excuse to do it and not be disciplined. So imagine my surprise when I was now being made accountable for my actions. Consequences followed acting out. I had no idea what she was trying to do; nevertheless, I loved her for it. At least she was trying and I felt like she was paying attention to me.

I had continued to use awful language in everyday conversation, even with adults; but quickly learned this was no longer acceptable. Mommy commanded a certain level of respect without ever asking directly for it. It was an unspoken understanding. I really respected her and her opinions and never wanted to do anything that disappointed her. Just the thought of it sent a wave of caution through me. I wanted to be certain not to mess anything up this time. I needed this placement to work, and it had to be the last. I wanted a mother more than anything in the world and she wanted the job. I was smart enough to know that if you want to sell a product, you have to display it in a manner that makes the customer want to try it. So, I made sure to put my best foot forward.

One more change would have rocked me to the core. I don't think my heart could have handled it. Forget my heart, I could not take it. I would break into a million pieces. As it turns out, my mom had no preconceived notions about who I was. She just wanted me to try to be happy. She wanted to help me reclaim life as a child. What did that mean? I could not recall "carefree-childlike" days. I did not know how to go from an adult to a kid. For many years, I had taken care of myself and now Mommy wants me to be a kid. I gave it a shot. It seemed I had nothing to loose and everything to gain.

Surviving the Storm {72}

After adjusting to a curfew, telling my mom where I was going and not being so temperamental, I moved onto the next challenge - anorexia. To deal with my anorexia meant I had to deal with the root of the issue - self esteem. When was I going to learn to love myself? Somehow there was a connection with loving myself and learning to eat on a daily basis.

Prior to moving in with Lorraine, I probably ate only three times a week. Now my goal was to try to eat everyday of the week. This was one of the hardest things I have ever tried to do. If I had to do it alone, I would have surely failed. I had help. Mommy and I figured out creative ways to teach me that food was not my enemy and although eating is still an everyday struggle, it does not consume my life.

The real issue was I felt ugly. In fact, I sub-consciously surrounded myself with beautiful people. I felt that if I was around these people I would somehow get their beauty. In reality, I achieved the exact opposite. I began to resent the people around me. People often say that in the circle of your friends there is usually one ugly ducking. There was no mistaking the fact that I was the "ugly duckling" of my group. That eye-opener caused me to retreat. I knew I could not hide behind these people forever. I had been teased and called ugly and black all my life. I was hoping that if people saw me with beautiful people, they would consider me beautiful too.

I can remember someone telling a story about a foreign car that he was trying to have repaired domestically. The car needed a new part and after some shopping around he decided to try to have the part replaced with its domestic equal in order to reduce the total amount of his bill. When he went to the mechanic he was informed that the man was not equipped to replace the part that he needed. He was then told that in order to restore the car to working order he needed to go directly to the manufacturer. He needed to go to the original maker of the car because the maker would be able to replace the part with no problem. I was the foreign car and my heart was damaged. There had been some irreparable damages done to my heart by the people I loved. In order to restore my heart to working order I could not look to a superficial method of repair (food). I had to use what had damaged my heart to fix it... love, my newly defined experiences with love.

I could not hide the fact that my heart had absorbed some pretty hard knocks. What I really needed was to be reminded of how true love feels. You know what I mean by true love; the love that stays up late at night when I am sick. I needed the type of love that would cheer for me at every basketball and volleyball game. I wanted the love that would come to math class with me when I was failing and learn what I was learning at the same time so that I could get a higher grade. I knew what I wanted and needed when it came to love, but somehow I thought I was asking for too much. I also thought that if I could recognize true love in action everyday, then I would go to it and escape situations where there was not true love.

I know that perfect love is almost impossible to achieve, yet I believed in the possibility. I had faith and hope that this love would heal my heart and I could learn to love myself. Love is patient and kind. It does not seek out bad in people, but rather rejoices in the goodness of others. Love does not brag or gossip; it isn't rude or easily angered, and it keeps no record of wrong doing. Love always trusts, always protects, and always hopes. In short, love never fails. Imagine the difficulty I faced trying to find true love when my life had been ruined by those who were supposed to love me. I wanted love so badly that it hurt. It seemed that in order to experience true love, I had to learn to love myself first.

So the most difficult task still waits... to love myself. I had convinced myself for years of why I was not worthy of love. Now, I struggle to believe the opposite. I kept trying to persuade myself that I could handle it, but I was weak and lacked faith in myself. I had been stripped of the innate strength that I once embodied simply because I was a "Charles." I needed more than just my last name in order to win this battle. For years I was told that I was too black, skinny, and ugly, and it had finally gotten to me. I believed those things. I hated my dark skin. I was called "Blacky" for a number of years. I remember the confidence my sister had and I wanted it. Why didn't I have that Charles confidence? I started to hate being separated from my siblings, especially my sister. I needed her. I missed living in the same house with someone that shared the same name as me.

Being a Charles had become a hassle. It was not the Charles that bothered me. In fact I loved being a Charles. My identity had been wrapped up in my name, yet foster care did not allow me to maintain those biological connections. I was separated from my siblings for a number of years. My sister and I rarely spoke and I never talked with my brothers. I was unable to see my sister and brothers for years, so naturally I had some identity issues. It didn't matter to the rest of the world that I was a Charles because they were unaware of the reputation attached to the name; truthfully, even I was starting to forget. I struggled to remember the look of my siblings. My memory of my brothers began to fade along with the night we all moved into foster care. The night that changed our lives forever; I wanted to forget it, but not my brothers. How could I start loving myself apart from my siblings?

I was told that each person was created with care to be special and different from all others. Was I hand-woven or pieced together? I considered a person who weaves cloth or assembles electronic equipment. All of the intricate details that he or she must consider before they begin. They specifically choose each piece, how it fits with the others to equally contribute to the splendor and purpose of the finished work. Is that really how it was for me? Was each part of me specifically designed? Was it meant for me to have this exact shaped face, the dimple on my cheek, the curve of my nose, and the chocolate tone of my skin?

It has taken a long time for me to become comfortable in my own skin. It took patience and practice and letting people into my circle. After I started to love myself a little at a time, it became easier to love people around me. I became secure. I no longer believed that the people around me had ulterior motives when they told me that I was beautiful. I still do not accept compliments well, but at least I no longer feel like the entire world was telling a joke and I was the universal punch line.

It has taken literally years to get here, but I am here and I am happy. I was twenty-one years old before I understood and believed in my beauty. It is an internal belief, rarely impacted by external features. I felt so liberated from the prison of low self-esteem. It is still difficult to eat everyday because not eating is my comfort zone for when life gets chaotic. I am purposeful in my quest to stay healthy. I have good weeks and bad weeks. But for the first time ever in life, I love me! Can you believe that? I actually love me.

The hardest test I had was to fall in love with what I see in the mirror on a daily basis. I never thought it would happen and it has. I expect I will continue to have good and bad days. Nature teaches that universal truth; even on stormy, rainy days, the sun can come out and dominate. The positive force will win out in time. Allow faith and hope to help you believe you are worth love…real love.

EPILOGUE
Storm chasers

The beauty of the storm is endurance. By enduring storm after storm, you can begin to develop a familiarity with the atmospheric conditions prior to its arrival. Then it becomes your responsibility to be aware of any changes in the atmosphere that suggest a storm maybe brewing. You become, more or less, a meteorologist tracking the storms of life and setting provisions in place for survival.

However, storms are not always unpredictable. They can be tracked, preparations can be made, and people can survive depending on their place in the storm. Handling a storm takes skill, obedience, respect, experience, and adherence to protocol and understanding your options. You don't have to be a storm chaser to learn and appreciate what it takes to survive a storm. They will happen without looking. The storms you face can enhance your character, prepare you for future goals, and build self-confidence if you let them. They can also influence the lives of others you touch and enrich your developing life.

It was July 2005 and I was a college student. Mommy and her husband were expecting their first child in August. She and I sat in the living room reminiscing about the good old days. Then she asked if she could adopt me. I was ecstatic! I wanted to be a part of her family for so long and now she suggested we actually make it legal. Mommy had asked before, but we decided that it would be better to wait. While there were several great reasons to wait, one reason involved facing my biological family. I did not want to explain to them why I wanted Lorraine to be my mother. I knew I would have to provide more details than I wanted. But on that day, with all of my fears and uncertainty, I finally said yes. My fears and uncertainty were now joined with excitement and a feeling of finally becoming whole.

Before long, Mommy and I went down to the Guildford County Courthouse to file the petition for an adult adoption. I could not believe it was finally happening. My happiness only lasted a moment when I looked down at the list of things that were needed to complete the adoption. I needed to contact my biological mother and tell her that I intended to be adopted. I was angry when I read the list. I was required to write a letter outlining my intentions to be adopted and where she could contest the adoption if she desired. It made no sense to me that I had to contact the woman who did not even want me and essentially ask her permission to be adopted. All of the feelings of rejection came rushing back and overtook me. I was not ready to face her. What if she contested the adoption? What if she made this into a long drawn out process? I would just die if she caused me any more unnecessary pain.

I went to work and wrote a letter to my biological mother. I knew I had to do it quickly; otherwise I would loose my nerve. The letter read as if a professional had written it. I emailed the letter to Mommy to get her opinion. I wanted to make sure I was not too harsh. After getting her opinion, I printed and mailed the letter. My heart raced as I thought of what she would say to me. The letter had to be sent certified mail; which meant that she had to sign for the letter. This provided a record for both the court and I to know that she had received it. I tried to imagine what it would be like for her to receive my letter. Would she hate me even more? Would she somehow understand that this is what I need? Would she even care? I never wanted to hurt her and I wanted to make sure she knew that.

I could not stand the waiting. When I got home that I night I decided to call my biological mother to let her know what I had decided. My stomach was turned in knots and I just knew I would throw up waiting for her to answer the phone. When she finally answered, I told her she would receive a letter from me, explained what it said, and that I just wanted to be adopted. She was very cold to me, as I had expected. After struggling through a one-sided, five minute conversation with her, I told her that I loved her and would always love her, but I had to do this for me. I remember wanting her to say she loved me too. She has never said that to me and my heart wanted to hear it badly. She said nothing. She hung up the phone and that was it. I was prepared for her harshness; for the cold tone, but I was not prepared to still feel empty. The familiarity of the emptiness filled me. I was quickly transported to my childhood days of loneliness and abuse. I just sat there on my bed and cried. I was so upset that I got physically sick. I cried late into the night. I knew this would happen, yet it hurt anyway. There was apparently no way to prepare for this storm. It was unpredictable and yet predictable all at the same time. It was nearly a week before I smiled again.

The adoption process was more waiting than anything else. We continued with our everyday lives and learned not to think much about it. Then on December 30, 2005, I received a phone call from someone at the Guilford County Courthouse, while shopping with my friends. The woman told me she had something I should pick it up as soon as possible. It was nearly five in the evening; the courthouse would soon close. I rushed to the courthouse. The woman handed me a gold envelope and I left. I waited to get home before I opened it.

When I walked in the door, Mommy was waiting for me. I handed her the envelope and we sat on the sofa. There was a white piece of paper with bold lettering across the top, it read: DECREE OF ADULT ADOPTION. Those words hit us like a ton of bricks. Was this finally real? Was I really adopted? Is Mommy really my Mommy? She and I sat and read all of the implications of this decree. It basically said I was hers and she was mine…forever! I could not believe this one piece of paper had the ability to make me whole. I was floored. I could not stop staring at Mommy all day. Although my heart wished I could have had this feeling sooner, it was still worth it to experience it now. All of the hurt, the pain, the long suffering, and the waiting were worth it in that one moment. I did not realize how powerful this moment would be. Wow!

I knew that being adopted would upset some people, but this time, I had to do what I needed to do for me. For once in my life, I made a decision purely for me and my family. I am pleased to report it was the right decision. If I had gone into the adoption process thinking and believing my biological mother would never hurt me again, and would magically start loving me, the process would have been overwhelming.

Storm Chasers anticipate the eventual storm and prepare themselves to handle it. Emotionally, it was a tough process because I had to sever ties with my biological mother all the while still loving her. I learned that it is possible to love and leave her. I am not certain if she will ever love me the way I love her, but I do not care about that anymore. All that I suffered at her hand is not worthy of comparison to the amazing life I have now. Everyday that I get to call my mom, Mommy, is a great day and I am thankful that the storm was worth it.

BEYOND THE STORM

By Nancy Carter, ACSW

This next section is intended for both individuals and groups to learn and grow from Julia's story. While sharing her story around the country, she has been received with compassion and met with inquiries such as, "What can we do?" Both youth and adult audiences have responded to her advice, suggestions, and insight, and this section of her book is written to help move youths and adults to positively influence the lives of others and reach beyond the "storm." Julia believes that her experiences are written in vain unless they can help another.

Julia's advice is provided in each area of this section along with discussion questions, suggestions for training, and group activities. The specified audiences include youths, parents and caregivers, and social workers and other youth serving professionals; however, most readers will find the reflective questions allow them to re-consider personal and professional development goals.

Numbers by Julia offers a quick glance at Julia's life as defined by numbers. Statistical numbers do provide information about a person however; comprehensive understanding of an individual can be lost if only the numbers are evaluated. Julia's numbers (and your own) may not speak to the resiliencies developed through hope.

Youth Talk provides some advice for youths along with ideas for group activities. The activities can be promoted by youths or their adult advisors. All the activities are intended to provide a reflective experience and build youths' resiliencies. An adult advisor should be prepared and realize that both the discussions and activities can provide therapeutic benefits, and allow ample time for processing.

Advice for Parents and Caregivers provides grounded reminders that adults living with youths have significant influence on young people and their decisions.

Advice for Social Workers and Professionals can be helpful to any youth serving professionals who want to improve their relationships with young people. Julia's reminders have helped rekindle the passion for many social workers who have grown weary on their career paths.

NUMBERS BY JULIA

Young people in foster care often define themselves by "numbers;" number of placements, number of foster parents, number of years in foster care, etc. Despite the "numbers," Julia found ways to survive her storm. Below is a glance at Julia's life in terms of "numbers."

Years

In kinship care	9
In foster care	10
With biological mother	2

Days

She felt good about herself	5
She wished she was not alive	729

Things

Placements	16
School changes	9
Attended court hearings	0
Run away events	6
Academic awards	5

People

Foster parents	19
Biological siblings	11
Foster siblings	30
Social workers	7
Friends	3
Boyfriends	5
People she could count on	1
People she physically hurt	36
People who physically hurt her	7
Visits with the principal	25
Visits with the police	2

Discussion question for all groups

What numbers do you think helped Julia survive?

What numbers do you think negatively impacted Julia?

What do your numbers say about your resiliencies?

Are there areas where you would like to increase your numbers?

YOUTH TALK

Been there. Done that.

You've heard it before and listened to other foster youths.

Now it's time to listen to you…. What does Julia's story tell you about YOU?

Although everyone's situation is different, there are some general things you can do FOR YOURSELF that will help you survive the foster care system.

When you do leave foster care, remember, it does not mean all the issues go away. In fact, it may mean that it's time to deal with them…maybe for the first time.

Reconnect with other foster youth and alumni via websites or community meetings. It may make the difference in your survival.

Listen

Listen to your foster parent(s); even if you do not trust them, listening can make your stay in their homes a lot smoother.

Listen to your social workers; even if you do not like them, they may be a valuable resource for you.

Listen to other foster youths, they might say some things you need to hear or you might be able to make a difference in their lives.

Trust

While it is not a good idea to trust everyone, it is important to trust someone. Trust, even in the smallest amount, helps build healthy relationships.

Get Educated

Education is the key to success. College is not for everyone, but education is important and available to everyone. If you do not want to go to college, learn a trade and do it to the best of your ability. Just continue your education even into adulthood.

Get a Hobby

Whether it's reading or sports; hobbies help occupy your mind when other stuff is going on; depending on the hobby, it can also help cultivate valuable life skills.

Make an agreement

Check out the adults in your life. Identify those you respect and trust.

Make an agreement or contract, with one or more of them, that states you will do your best but that you need their support.

All youths should have a significant adult permanently in their lives. Don't restrict yourself to just one though; the more the merrier.

Suggested Activities

1 At your next independent living meeting, consider discussing each of the items below and why group members think these may be important.

2 Research foster youth groups on the Internet and begin communicating.

3 Visit trade, vocational, community colleges, and four-year colleges to learn how education can be a part of adulthood.

4 Find a free local community event that your foster teen group can attend.

5 Make a list of up to five caring adults who you trust.

6 Ask to be a part of foster parent recruitment and training to help prepare foster homes to accept teens into their homes.

7 Make a list of your "numbers" (see Numbers by Julia, page 84), those numbers that help you and those that challenge you. What have you learned about your ability to survive your storm?

8 Discuss in a group how your "storm" is shaping you. Consider how you might help calm or "stir up" the storm. What opportunities did a previous storm provide that you would not have had otherwise? Did that experience help you through the next storm?

If you want to write Julia, send an email to info@ilrinc.com and mark the subject "for Julia."

ADVICE FOR PARENTS AND CAREGIVERS

Upon reflection, Julia sees that she has had both good and bad foster parents. She's also been in kinship care and ultimately an adoptive home. She has also been actively involved in foster parent training. Her experiences and advice are realistic and grounded.

Relax
Youths may not want a hug or a kiss as soon as they come through the door, but it does not mean they hate you; just relax and allow them to approach you.

Relate
You may not relate to a young person's situation exactly, but you were once young too. Try to relate in that regard; this will let the young person know you are interested without trying to become a friend.

Listen
Listen to youths. They just might share things that give you greater insight into who they are and what they like. Connect with them in areas of mutual interests.

Learn
Learn as much as you can about being a foster parent. Even if you already have biological children and have that "parenting thing down pat," recognize that foster parenting is another ball game.

Love

Your method to show love for a youth should not be contingent upon whether the young person loves you back. Do your part and love each youth anyway.

Let Go

After you have done all the relaxing, relating, listening, learning, and loving that you can do, let go. It is important to know when to let go and allow young people to stand on their own feet. It's also okay to miss them when they are gone; and for them to miss you.

Training Suggestions

1 Reflect on each of the above qualities. Consider relationships that contain these qualities. How are you different with those relationships versus those without these qualities?

2 List ways to demonstrate the qualities Julia suggests. Explore how you can improve your relationship with the young people in your home by practicing those behaviors.

3 Ask the young people what you could do in each category that would help them believe you care about them.

4 List various analogies (storm, eye, potter, etc.) offered by Julia and discuss how your experiences with young people reflect those analogies.

ADVICE FOR SOCIAL WORKERS/PROFESSIONALS

Julia's personal and professional experiences with social workers have led her to now understand social workers and other youth serving professionals. Her advice is meant to be a reminder of your professional role in helping develop youth's preparedness for self-sufficiency while keeping them safe.

Listen

Listen to foster parents because they live with the youths. Ask clarifying questions and listen carefully to their responses to help you understand the situation.

Listen to the young people because it's their lives.

SaySo* has a saying, "don't let them create policy and plans about you without you." Practice (nothing about them, without them) by actively listening.

Learn

Try to gain as much knowledge about your field as you possibly can because it can be your most valuable asset. The field of social work changes rapidly - stay informed and pass information on to others. Do not keep it to yourself.

Teach

It is important to teach others what you have learned; share knowledge with your co-workers and other professionals. Teach and support caregivers. Teach youths how to build competencies. Remember, you learned your skills for a reason.

---

*SaySo (Strong Able Youth Speaking Out) is a youth advocacy organization in North Carolina for current and former foster youths. Julia has been a member for many years.

Remember

Remember why you came into this field of work. It is very likely that you started in this field of work because a part of you cared about youths and families. Maybe an experience or a person prompted your concern. Maybe, remembering why you started on this career path will inspire you.

Let Go

After you have done all that you can it is important to let go; let foster parents do their jobs and let youths stand on their own two feet. Once youths have the tools, let them make decisions and build their world.

Training Suggestions

1 Create a series of five training sessions using each topic as the focus.

2 Discuss the storm analogy Julia uses. Have staff reflect on the personal and professional storms that have shaped them and their clients.

3 Discuss how "numbers" impact youths (see Numbers by Julia, page 84). Brainstorm ways to minimize youths' academic and placement transitions.

4 Ask each staff member to contract for behavioral changes that influence how the topics are practiced.

ACKNOWLEDGEMENTS

First to my friend, my love, my passion, my peace, my King, my redeemer, and my provider Jesus Christ, thank you for everything. I love you more than anything in this world. Thank you choosing me to endure this battle for the Glory of your name.

To the late Legolia Lee (Grandma), I miss you so much. Life has not been the same without you.

To Mommy, I will let you know that you are my hero because heroes have their own lives, yet they show up just in-the-nick-of-time to rescue others in a supernatural way. I thank God for using you to rescue me. I love you more than you'll ever know.

To my brother Isaiah, I love you very much!

To the late Delbra Diane Alston, I thank you for your patience and not giving up on a very rebellious me. Kareem, for loaning your mother to me so unselfishly, I thank you.

To Mrs. Dawn Jordan, I love you more (I win!)

To Nancy Carter, thank you for believing in me and all the other youth in care.

To Samantha Powell-Jones and Michelle Studmire I love you! You are the best friends ever.

Vince and Cheryl Hairston, I couldn't ask for a better lead. I love you both.

"Real Ministry, For Real Life, For Real People," what an awesome way to serve God's people!

To Belinda Smith and all of the LINKS teens, thank you.

And finally, to every young person that has ever been in foster care for whatever reason, this is for you.

Love,
Julia S Charles

REORDER FORM

Order online at www.ilrinc.com, call or by mail

919-384-1457 | 1-800-820-0001 | fax 919-384-0338

Surviving the Storm

By Julia Charles (#096)

_____ copies x $11.95 = $_____

NC residents add 6.75% sales tax = $_____

Shipping and handling @ 8% = $_____
$6 minimum

Total $_____

Make payment to
ILR, Inc.
411 Andrews Road, Suite 230, Durham, NC 27705
(FEIN ID # 56-1579837)

q MC q VISA

Name on card

Phone number

Card number   Expiration date

Ship to:

Visit www.ilrinc.com for more information about
Surviving the Storm and other resources.